these
TIPS
were made for
TALKING

SELLING & MANAGEMENT
TECHNIQUES

Leja,
Hope you enjoy the book!

these
TIPS
were made for
TALKING

SELLING & MANAGEMENT
TECHNIQUES

JIM THOMPSON

TATE PUBLISHING & Enterprises

ISBN: 1-5988669-9-0
06.09.14

I'd like to express special thanks to my wife, Pat, for her enduring support in writing this book.

There are so many friends and family members who also supported this venture. Words cannot express my admiration and respect for my co-workers and management at Aflac where I had the privilege of working the past 30 years.

A special mention of gratitude goes to the South Territory field force at Aflac. Together we made it happen!

I also want to thank my publishers, Tate Publishing, who allowed me the opportunity to share my "Tips" with everyone.

Personally, I feel that is what life is all about - - sharing and caring for others and watching each other succeed. Hopefully, these tips will help everyone in reaching their goals.

TABLE OF CONTENTS

INTRODUCTION

"Here goes another one," you are thinking as you turn to this first page. Let's see if I can guess. You're thinking, "Here's another book about sales and management that will ask the same old questions and then try to explain them," such as "How to close a sale", "How to deal with objections", et cetera, saying the same things as other books with a few different words. Maybe so, maybe not. I've read many of them - I know what you mean. But they have been very helpful to me, both personally and in business.

I don't really know how to describe this book except to say, "Fellow sales persons - fellow managers - here's what I have learned and experienced in sales and management."

For a guide, I have furnished the normal "Table of Contents" to list the subjects we will cover. Don't let the titles fool you. Sometimes there's just no other title to be used. Read each chapter - see if it hits home.

There are a few other things I want you to remember while "enjoying" this book.

1. A lot of people have the idea that all great sales people were born that way. Either you've got it or you don't. Don't believe it! It just isn't so.
   a. Remember - Anyone can learn how.
   b. For everyone - there's always room for improvement.
2. While the book is not just entertainment - because making money is serious - the information is lightly flavored in order for you to take small doses and enjoy it more.
3. Nothing in this book will do you any good unless you do something about it. That's the catch. You will be on the spot to perform. Use it or lose it.
4. The more that things change in the business of selling, the more they stay the same.
   The book is written to:
   1. Say what really works.
   2. Get back to basics.
   3. Target key areas we need to review to make sure we are back to the basics.
   4. Be honest with ourselves.
   5. Make us better sales people and sales managers.

Enjoy!

DO YOU HAVE TIME?

Living in Georgia, I probably could play golf about seventy-five percent of the year on weekends. The weather normally will permit that, which is great.

Several years ago, a friend asked if I had been playing golf lately. I replied, without hesitation, "Well, you know I travel quite a bit and I just haven't had time to play golf." End of statement. Have you heard that statement before? "I haven't had the time." I had the time; I just did not use the time I did have playing golf. It was used in some other activity. I want to share with you in this chapter why we should never use time as an excuse. If we do, we're just kidding ourselves and lying. Now, when I'm asked the question, "Jim, have you played golf lately?" and I haven't, I say, "No, I just haven't taken the time to play golf. I used the time doing other things, but I do have the time, would you like to play Saturday?" In other words, we all have the time; it's up to us to use it properly.

Let's see, how many hours are there in a year available to use, 25,600 hours or 26,500 hours? Which do you say? If you guessed either, you're the ultimate optimist. Actually, there are 8,760 hours in a 365-day year. Seems like just a few, doesn't it? Let's take a look at how these hours are spent.

Let's assume, that out of the 365 days in the year, we will take 104 days for weekends, 14 days vacation, 5 sick, 22 for other activities, which leaves us with 220 days to actually work. Let's just assume that is reasonable and realistic.

The following is diagram #1 (all of these type books have to have at least one diagram) to show how we use our time each day (assuming you will agree with the figures I've used). I have asked many sales people and sales managers and these are very close to what they came up with during this mathematical exercise.

Question	how many days involved	Results in hours
How may hrs. per day Do you work	7 X 200 Days	1,540
How many hrs. per day Do you eat	2 hrs. X 365	730
How many hrs. per day Do you sleep	8 X 365	2,920
How many hrs. per day Do you entertain or play	3 X 365	1,095
How many hrs. per day Do you spend on Misc	1 X 365	365
		6,650 hours

These activities cover the actual things that probably have to be done and we've probably used more hours then necessary on some activities. You know how we can waste our time.

Now, we started off with 8,760 hours, we've used 6,650 hours, which means there's 2,110 hours left in the year to do other things. That calculates to be about 5.78 hours per day that we have available to do other things than mentioned in this exercise. Almost six hours a day - twenty-five percent of the twenty-four hour day. How can we use those words, "I don't have enough time"? I think we've just proven that the time is there. It's up to us to use it, the way we want to and choose to.

You can't turn back the clock,
But you can sure wind it up again

Now that we've established the fact that we do have enough time, what do we do now? Well, let's wind ourselves up and start ticking. You ask yourself how, "How do I want to use my time?" Get yourself a piece of paper and pen. List all the important things you have done within the past twenty-four hours and note beside each one, the time it took to do these things. Yes, just pause for a few minutes - put this book down, and start listing your past twenty-four hour accomplishments and how much time it took.

Now, don't include eating or house cleaning, or going to the laundry, and miscellaneous things we do each day. I mean the things that you feel are special accomplishments, like solving some business or personal problems, making headway on a special project, helping a friend, helping your company through a special act of yours - you know the things which you would do if you had the time.

What, you've finished already! How much time did you spend doing these things? If you are the average person, your list won't be very long and the time you spent was a flash. If you are an organized executive, salesperson, or sales manager, you are probably surprised to see that your list is not as long as you thought it was and the time you spent was not as great as you thought it was. How about it?

Again, this exercise should prove and show you that we need to spend more time on more important things. We have the time. We just sometimes let it pass by as if it were lost in space with no value being placed on it.

You've wound yourself up. Now start ticking and be conscious of all the time you do have to do things you need to do and want to do, but never thought you had the time to do them.

Best wishes to you and all your time.

"ORGANIZATION" OR "WHAT DO I DO NEXT?"

"To Do Or Not To Do" - that is the question which haunts every new sales person, experienced sales person, new manager, experienced manager, wife, husband, or children.

In all the meetings I've attended with sales people, a major problem, universal in every walk of life, is the organization of things you need and want to accomplish and being able to prioritize them. Most of the time we spend a great effort in trying to decide where to start to get things done.

How simple it seems when we go back to some basics we've heard about, read about, and even tried before. Remember when it worked last time you did it? You're asking now "Remember when what worked?" Okay, here it goes again - but this time believe it and do it. Do it for ninety straight days.

"To Do" things in an organized way
with priorities I recommend that you:

- Make two separate lists each day on the same sheet of paper. (You may use your notebook if you wish.)
- On one side, list your definite appointments, meetings, and other items with a specific time schedule.
- On the other side, make your "To Do" list - things needing to be accomplished that day or calls you wish to make other than the ones listed in #2 above.
- Review the "To Do" list and number or place them in a priority "To Do" order.
- Then review both lists to make sure the activity you plan is consistent with the goals you have on a short term and long term basis.
- Work your list.
- Any hold-overs may be transferred and placed properly on the next day's list. One caution, if you find yourself continually placing an item on the next day's list, you might have a case of "procrastination."
- Make your list at least one night before the next day's activity.

How many times have some of us heard the basics of making a list to get and keep organized? Another question, "How many people do you know who use these basics", and out of those, "How many are successful people?" Most successful people have lists with priorities.

Another effective tool is called a "log book". This has been especially helpful to new sales people as an organizational tool and to sales managers as a management tool. You'll be amazed when I tell you what it consists of in the raw form and how simple a tool it is to be so effective.

Here's the best description I can give of the "log book" and the advantages of this tool. A regular composition notebook (about $2.98) is the only raw material needed. Then:

- Number 1 through 20 on each page for 60 pages.
- Date each page with day and date. (This will carry you through approximately three months of work days - 5 days/1 week.)
- The numbers 1 through 20 are to list the calls you want to make that day (list them at least the night before). Use names and addresses.

    After each call, make a note beside name, and what happened.

    Did you make the sale?

    What did you sell?

Did you see the people to make a presentation?
If not, what was the reason or objection?

In other words - what happened "activity-wise" on this call?

- At the top of each page make some notations regarding your mileage starting and ending the day: Expenses incurred, stamps, and any other items for record.

- Any calls not made that day or any call-backs needed may be entered on future pages under the correct day and date.

Phone--$1.00
Wednesday
Stamps- 39 cents   2-11-06

| 1. John Doe-111 Sam St. Detroit Sold X and Y. |
| 2. Mary Doe- 111 Sam St. Detroit not home 2:30 pm at work –call back at 5:00pm |
| 3. Sue Moss—113 Sam St. Detroit –gave pres.-no sale |

39219----40,220 Mileage
Phone $1.00
Thursday   2-12-06

| 1. Mary Doe 111 Sam St. Detroit Saw at 6:00 pm Sold A&B |
| 2. etc. |
| 3. etc. |

What does the log book do for you?

- Provides organization for salesperson.
- Has a plan.
- Does not waste time trying to decide where to go.
- Provides record showing activity.
- Provides record of expenses and mileage for IRS on commission sales people and information for activity reports for others.
- Provides information for both salesperson and manager to review to see where improvement is needed or to spot any problem areas in closing - getting in the door, et cetera.
- Helps salesperson plan future activities more effectively using information from logbook.
- Show total activity at a glance.
- Provides your "To Do" items.
- Simple, un-complicated personal record.

What an inexpensive tool to do so much!

Of course, a current day daytimer book or computer calendar can accomplish the same thing. It doesn't matter which one you use, just use it.

The making of a list using the logbook approach or the daytimer and or computer has helped the most successful people become organization-oriented and always knowing what needs to be done and where their priorities are placed.

So, no more coffee drinking in the doughnut shop to think about what you will do today, right? I'm not against coffee and doughnuts, but if you plan to stop there, put it on the list!

"Procrastination"

I mentioned a disease called procrastination earlier and I want to include a short cure for this disease under this section on organization. This is done simply because I think procrastination is one of the real enemies of organization. To explain why I say this, I will use an example: You have just read about how lists will help you in organization. Some of you will procrastinate and delay using the log book or day timer/computer approach and will not improve organizing yourself. I challenge you to implement this cure. It's called the balance sheet method.

1. On the left side of a sheet of paper, list all the reasons you're procrastinating.
2. On the right side, list all the benefits that you will accomplish if you do something.

How many excuses do you have on the left side? And how much longer and important to you are the benefits on the right side, especially the benefit of relief. Enough said. You're cured!

Well, we could go on and on about organization and how to be better organized, but I want to move on to more subjects, ideas, and thoughts which I hope will help you.

Remember, "To Do or Not To Do" is often the question. We all know "To Do" is what we want and I hope I've helped you put another priority on your LIST, and I hope you "LOG" in your mind not to let procrastination keep you from becoming more ORGANIZED.

CONFIDENCE - WHERE ARE YOU WHEN I NEED YOU?

The fluttering heart, empty stomach, difficult breathing, and sweaty palms are not just rookie experiences salespeople go through before approaching a performance. Even experienced salespeople have some of these when involved in a situation where they do not feel up to par on their sales approach. Most of us have some form of excitement or nervousness every time we approach a sale, speech, or some public performance. This is natural, and good for us. It keeps us geared up and actually helps our performance.

Some of you have a difficult time in every sales or management situation. You get every symptom, and have difficulty dealing with them. You end up struggling through sales approaches, speeches and at management meetings. I feel this has a lot to do with lack of confidence in yourself to perform adequately in a particular situation.

Now "Lack of Confidence" is a broad area to discuss. Is it "Lack of Confidence" in the way you look, feel, sell, walk, talk, eat, or what? As far as selling and managing goes, let's discuss an area I have found to be the most prominent culprit of the "Lack of Confidence" syndrome. I call it "Fear of the Unknown" or lack of knowledge of the total situation at hand. Some of the first speeches I ever gave to groups of salespeople and managers were not up to par. The delivery was shaky - enthusiasm completely deserted - subject material researched, but fear made me forget several topics. All the nervous symptoms were present including a shaky voice. Why? Lack of knowledge - "Fear of what my audience would think". "No Confidence" because of "Lack of Knowledge" or "Fear of the Unknown".

I decided to speak to a speech expert to get advice. This expert gave this point. Whenever you speak, know what you are talking about. Know more about the subject than the audience. Study for weeks on the subject before the speech. Use your own words to speak about the subject. If you know your subject, you'll feel comfortable talking about it and your confidence in delivery will strengthen. Get someone to listen to you and critique you! Well for the next few speeches, I took that advice. I studied my subject matter and spent weeks composing a 20 minute talk. It was amazing. The flutters were still there initially and still are to this day; however, they do disappear about 10 seconds into the speech because "I know what I'm talking about now." What I share with others through speeches, I have studied, tested, and proven. I have confidence in my ability to deliver the message to the audience. Many people since then have been kind enough to tell me of the change they have seen in my current messages compared to the initial ones, "without the knowledge" and "without the confidence".

Sales situations are the same. If you are not knowledgeable about your product, your service, your presentation, your rebuttals, your closes, you will most likely always have a "Lack of Confidence". In the business world, I have seen a lot of sales people and managers come and go. In counseling with many of them, I discovered that where a sales person fails, there usually is a failure in lack of total knowledge of the total sales techniques. For the manager, a failure accompanies lack of knowledge and use of management principles. I have been in the field with some of these sales persons, and observed their lack of study and knowledge of their company, product, or sales techniques. With managers, I have observed their lack of developing management skills and techniques that have been taught at seminars. The failures just did not attempt to develop the proper knowledge of their responsibilities and therefore had a "lack of confidence" to succeed because of "Lack of Knowledge" or "Fear of the Unknown".

You find the successful sales person, or the successful manager, and you'll find them knowledgeable about what they're doing and saying.

Summary

This chapter seems short on such a broad subject but again, I want to point out the one main cause for "Lack of Confidence"; it is "Lack of Knowledge". Here's some suggestions on how to get that "Knowledge".

- Know your company (statistics, profits, sales, goals).
- Believe in your company.
- Know your product; be able to give a presentation without materials, be able to read brochures upside down. Memorize your features and benefits.
- Believe in your product; buy your products. (However, you may not need a $50,000 paving machine for just your driveway).
- Research and study subjects for speeches three weeks before the speech. Make an outline and add to or delete from at least six times.
- Study your sales presentation until it flows from your lips like you are acting in a Shakespearian

play. It will allow you to place enthusiasm in the proper places.

- Study all rebuttals to objections and know them as well as the main part of your presentation.
- Get someone to listen to your speech in advance.
- If you get to be an expert speaker, please change your themes in a timely manner and watch the jokes.

Have confidence that you know where your confidence lies.

So if you now have the confidence that your knowledge and organization will give you, take the time to look at what lies ahead . . .

Enthusiastically toward Chapter 4.

DO YOU REALLY HAVE SOMETHING TO SELL?

This short chapter is especially for the new sales-person. The above question is one you should ask yourself immediately. For those of you who have been selling a product for a while and still aren't doing too well, ask yourself the same question.

Going out knocking on those doors - meeting a different person every few minutes, some slamming the door in your face - can be frustrating to say the least. But the ones you get to listen to you are where you have your chance to put your product into their lives. Here's some things you need to help you make the sale.

First, a big, warm, sincere smile as you give your greetings. Then have the four following things in your mind. You must however believe them.

• Know that you have something that they need - something they ought to have.

- You have come there with something to give them.
- They are going to get something worth more than what they pay for it.
- You are not there to outdo them, but to give them something worthwhile.

Coupled with these four beliefs your attitude should be that you're going out to help the community.

In any selling situation, you should be selling something that is going to be a blessing to others. Something they need - you know they need it! And you're there to give it to them.

Find someone who needs you to tell them about your product. Help them!

This chapter was short, but hopefully will bring you rewards for a long time.

WHERE ARE YOU GOING?

Goals To Find The Way

I read somewhere about an executive who said, "The important thing is not where you were or where you are, but where you want to get."

Human progress, inventions, medical discoveries, and triumphs of all kinds were first visualized, then became realities. Space travel is not an accident; it's an accomplished goal, not a dream. Goals are dreams being acted upon.

Certain questions are usually asked of successful people. One of the most popular questions is "What do you attribute as the reason for your success?" The standard answer to this popular question is "My ability to set goals and dedication to pursuing them with great desire." Don't you all agree that you've heard this said more than once? Being that goals are always on successful people's lists as being an item which helps them become successful, isn't it amazing how few people really set goals. And those who do, how few people follow them.

A fairly new associate with my previous company was discussing his future with me. He had been offered a management position in his state with our company and wasn't sure if that's what he wanted as a career. I recommended that we discuss his future in terms of looking at his thinking of what he wanted to be and where he wanted to be ten years from now.

He answered, "Well, like everyone else, I'd like to make a lot of money and have a nice home, but really I haven't given it much thought."

He felt confused at first until I mentioned that he was in the majority in that most people do not have a ten year plan or for that matter, there are quite a lot of people with no goals at all. Then I explained that he is having difficulty deciding on his career because, without goals, it's like going to a bus station and saying "Give me a ticket." The ticket seller can't help you unless you tell him where you want to go. It was hard for him to make the decision he was faced with, because he did not know what his destination was, and only he can decide that.

After that brief discussion on goals, we began talking about his future with our company ten years from now. He did not accept the position of manager at that time but he does have it as a goal and I believe now he does know where he wants to go.

"BIP" Your Goals"
Long Term Goals

Long-Term Goals and ten-year plans are accomplished when you "BIP" your goals. "BIP" is my slogan for "Breaking Into Pieces". "BIP" Long-Term Goals to develop the Short-Term Goals directing daily, weekly, monthly and yearly activity toward the Long-Term Goals. Why must you "BIP" your Long-Range Goals? It becomes easier to see your goals clearly and you end up getting things done.

Big things (Long-Term Goals) are accomplished "one step at a time" so you must "BIP" your goals so that they are easier to put together, easier to understand. A house is built a brick at a time. Any big accomplishment is just a series of little accomplishments.

"An hour is easy - forever is difficult"

Know where you're going and "BIP" your way. Then take one more step and the next page will take you closer to another Short-Term accomplishment of reading Chapter VI.

TELEPHONE - USED FOR - TALKING!

Telephone For Appointments To Sell

The first lesson and probably the main lesson to learn about using the telephone as a salesperson is that you should not try to make the sale over the phone. Your main purpose, if you are selling a product, is to get an appointment with the prospect to "Show and Tell". Unfortunately, at this time - even with the new teleconferencing systems - the sales pitch just doesn't work well over the phone. You might say that you're just wasting a good sales pitch if you try to sell over the phone.

For selling a product, the phone can be used very effectively to make the appointment. It can also be used very ineffectively if you do not use the correct phone techniques. Believe me, I've lost many appointments by not being aware that there are some basic techniques for using the telephone that make its use more effective. I've seen many salespeople blow the appointment but not using the correct telephone techniques. Okay, you're saying, let's hear them. What are some pointers on using the telephone for getting appointments to sell my products? Here are four points, again basic, easy to understand things that if you use them properly will improve your use of the telephone.

- Planning your phone conversation is an absolute must. Do not doubt it. The conversations are short and you have to know what you want to say - say it without a pause or delay and know how you want to say it. Gestures and movements of the hand, head, or eyes don't get it over the phone. Have your script and practice till it's a perfectly natural flow of words (not just read from paper).
- Sell the appointment - not your product. Most salespeople get so involved in telling about the product and this is a common mistake. The time for selling the product is face to face - not over the phone. Of course, you have to make the prospect interested in the product or service, but just an interest, not the whole sales pitch. You want the chance to tell your story in person - not over the phone.

- An addition to point #2 above is "Don't reveal too much." The prospect will ask several questions over the phone. "What is the price?" "How long will it last?" "Who else has purchased it?" I know that you know many more questions they ask to try to get all the information they can over the phone - trying to say "no" to you. Don't give them the answer. Just don't. Now, you can't be rude but you can learn several answers as part of your telephone script like "The prices vary according to the size and models, Mr. Jones, and that's why I need to show you exactly what I have," or "Mr. Jones, the acceptance of what I have to show you has been tremendous. I believe you'll be impressed and could see how it could benefit you also when you see all the features of our package. Would this week be convenient for you?"

- While the prospects - excluding any teleconference - can't see your head, eyes, and hands making gestures, they can detect and hear that smile in your voice. Your whole self is wrapped in that piece of plastic he has in his ear at the moment. That is you. Smile while you are talking. Be as pleasant as you can be. The prospect can see that smile even over the phone.

Now, those are just four short points to help you in making appointments for selling your products or services over the phone. There are more techniques, but if you will practice on just these four, it definitely will help you become more effective using the telephone.

BIG DECISIONS DON'T DETERMINE HOW OUR LIFE WILL BE

You probably realized you were in trouble when someone asked you that question, "You have a hard time making decisions, don't you?" And your reply was, "Yes and No!"

When people talk about decisions, they normally categorize them into big decisions, which make their life a certain way, and little decisions, which are looked at as rather insignificant. I stay amazed at the importance we place on "big decisions" in directing our life.

In other words, getting married wasn't the only decision. There were many small decisions made which had to be made to lead up to the so-called "Big one". My point is the many small decisions are really the important ones. They will determine what you finally decide in the end. They will make the difference. So place importance on them.

There are many decisions we make on a daily basis which affect our lives.

1. One may be to decide to put ourselves on the line.
2. To decide that sacrifice is part of the package when committing to something.
3. To decide to work harder, when we really feel like taking it easy.
4. To decide to turn our persistence loose.
5. To decide to go for #74 after 73 "No's".

Now again, those are not what we think of as "big decisions", but they certainly can make a drastic change in our lives, depending on how we treat them.

We have to make decisions to ask for what we want out of life. Decisions are just a part of everyday life and the daily decisions we make will add up to formulate what we think of as the Big decisions.

I hope you will make a decision to:

1. Turn your persistency loose
2. Put yourselves on the line
3. Receive your total share out of life.
4. And also make the decision to proceed to the next chapter.

IF THE BULL CAN PASS THE TEST
- SO CAN YOU

Even though I'm never been to a bullfight, I have heard people describe it to me. Once in Madrid, Spain, my wife and I, had an opportunity to attend a bullfight, but chose not to because of our love for animals. Our friends did go and some did give us the gory details. It is a sport and I'm sure it's very exciting to some people. I figured that the bulls had to be very ignorant to get stuck with the sword so many times and the matador had to be very brave.

After reading some information about the bulls selected for entrance into the arena with the matadors, I now know that both matador and bull are brave. It seems that in some countries, young bulls are tested before they are placed in an arena. The young bulls are placed into a ring with a "Picador" who proceeds to continually prick the young bull with a lance.

The bravery of the young bull is judged by how

often he demonstrates the willingness to attack in spite of the sting of the lance. Only the ones who demonstrate their "persistency" are termed "brave" enough to be placed in the ring with a matador.

As I was reading and thinking about this sport, I was reminded of how we are tested each day by life itself. Our ability and willingness to endure and be persistent is important to us if we want to succeed. We constantly have to be willing to face obstacles and go forward, just like the bull against the lance. What's that old saying, "You must persist until you succeed."

Have you ever thought about definitions for "persistency"? How about these?

1. Consider the postage stamp: Its usefulness consists in its ability to stick to one thing until it gets there.

Or:

2. Keep on going; nobody ever stumbles on anything sitting down.

Think about this question. I'm sure you will answer in the affirmative. "How many times have you been out selling or managing (still that's selling) and have really wanted to get up and go home, but something told you to keep going - try another call, have one more meeting, have that last interview and you do keep on - and, another success. Just think if you had quit that other success would have escaped you. But wasn't it fun to achieve that success by making that extra effort by being persistent.

Now if you've asked that question and the answer was "Never", run for help or either turn the next corner, make another step - you'll get there if you're persistent.

Cut Down the Oak Tree

Have you ever cut down a big oak tree with an ax? Or can you imagine it. The first big blow with the ax makes a small slice in the bark. The second blow starts a small opening by chipping off part of the bark. Both blows are felt only by our bodies - the tree does not budge. The third blow makes hardly any significant change in the progress of falling the tree. Then, as the blows continue to fall upon the tree, it becomes more apparent that this "big tree" will eventually crash to the earth, just as had been planned. The persistent blows with the ax finally falls the "big tree".

We can cut down our "big tasks" or "big goals". We can break them into pieces. Our consistent and persistent efforts will lead us - step by step - to our goals.

The Law of Average

Persistency in anything we do works along with

the "Law of average". Let the "Law of average" work for you in these ways.

- Each failure will increase your chance for success. Each "No" will bring you closer to a "Yes".
- Each frown prepares you for a smile.
- Be persistent and let the odds favor you.

One Step At a Time Is Not Difficult

Whatever our goals might be, whatever success we desire at any particular time we don't always know the exact timetable or system which will make everything fall exactly in place. We don't know the exact number of steps to take to reach our destination. Failures will probably jump out at every corner, but we never know how close we are to where we want to be until we turn the next corner. Another step must always be taken, then another, then another, then another. After all, we know that in truth, "One step at a time is not really difficult."

Sam Rawls, an insurance executive friend of mine, gave me this quote: "Life by the mile is a trial, life by the inch is a cinch, let's take an inch at a time."

May we not let yesterday's success lull us into complacency? May we greet today with the confidence and persistency that it will beat the best day of our lives. Remember the old Principle of Success, "If you persist long enough, you will win."

TODAY IS THE ONLY REAL LIFE DREAM

This chapter is dedicated to a business associate I met in Oregon. He provided me information which gave me the idea for these words and how true they are. Every sales person or manager must realize the importance of living for today.

How often we place our goals, our objectives, and our dreams in a position that suggests that when we reach them the bands will be playing, the flags waving, the end is there, we reached the final destination. What really happens as we approach that time - or when the dream has materialized? Do we stop there?

We find that, all of a sudden, there is no place to go at the end to become final, once and for all. The dreams, the goals, the objectives, constantly out-distance us. THE REAL JOY WAS IN THE TRIP.

But how often do we say "When I reach that goal, it will be the ultimate!" "When this dream comes true

I will be in heaven!" "If I can only get this sale made I will be set!" "I will live happily ever after!"

Then what happens? When we get "it", then "it" disappears. The end of the line constantly hides itself.

Yesterday and the fear of tomorrow is what really bothers us. They rob us of the exciting and present "today".

In summary, we must have our goals, our objectives, and our dreams; but only as places along the way, not as the final destination. Life must be lived as we go along.

So remember, this is not the end, just part of the way. The next chapter will carry you further.

CAN YOU SEE IT HAPPENING TO YOU?

Vision is helpful to us in many ways including being able to see something that is live before you, and real in your mind. Mental pictures are an important part of the motivating process when we are discussing the Power of the Mind.

If you are to achieve something in the future, you must be able to see it happening in your mind. Your mental vision must carry you through the process of doing it. For example, high jumpers usually picture themselves over and over again, jumping the heights they need to jump to win the competition. Their mind takes them through every step, then up in the air, over the bar, kicking that leg, and landing in the sawdust as they fall.

Let's discuss this Power of the Mind and how it's used in motivating ourselves. Again this will be relatively brief, but real.

Great achievers know what they want. They think about it. They see it. They know they will get it. If you will just think about the people you know or have read about who have broken records, you will find that the achievers probably told someone that he or she would achieve that record before even trying. They probably even mentioned a specific time period in which the goal would be achieved. Most great achievers also plan to achieve things which most people would term impossible. Here are three things that great accomplishers have in common. They tell people what they're going to do. They give a specific time. And they think in terms of accomplishing things others would think of as impossible.

My previous company had a special award that was presented to achievers during their first few months in sales if they produce at a certain level. A perfect example of achievers using the three steps mentioned above is three new sales associates I met at a regional outing in one of the western states. They came up to me after the meeting and told me they would achieve this award. Now, only about five percent or fewer of all the sales people the company hires each year, achieve this award. Also, it has to be achieved during a specific time period while the sales people are relatively new. If they miss the cut-off, it can never be achieved again.

These three, motivated, bright-eyed, opportunistic sales people knew what they wanted to do.
- They told someone.
- They had a specific time (They had no choice).
- It was difficult, something they had never achieved and although, not impossible, only five percent or less ever do it.

I think that's meeting all the criteria. Guess what! They did it. They could see it happening to them week-by-week, day-by-day, hour-by-hour; just like a high jumper visualizing the way they will make the jump and clear the bar. There was no doubt.

Can you see it happening to YOU? Can you envision your success using the Power of your Mind? Don't knock it till you've tried it. Also don't stop reading. Please go to the next page and let's look at another system designed to help you through the so-called "Slumps".

DISCIPLINE

This is a real key word in the sales person's life. It covers a lot of ground and disguised in many different forms.

Discipline of Studying
Discipline of Planning
Discipline of Time Management
Discipline of Making enough calls
Discipline of Communication
Discipline of Being Consistent
and on and on.

Discipline is very similar to the words practice, repetition, and rehearse because they all center around consistency and persistency in getting the job done.

What is the definition of discipline? Training that develops self-control efficiently.

In the sales person's mind, where does discipline count the most?

Everywhere!

- If you don't study and practice and rehearse - you waste a lot of time on calls. .
- If you don't plan - you waste time.
- If you don't manage well - you make less money than you should.
- If you don't make enough calls - you don't reach your potential.
- If a manager doesn't communicate - he or she doesn't really have enough information to help people effectively.
- Inconsistency keeps an organization or person working much harder to do the same job. Everything ties together!

For the sales people out there, the one *Real Big Thing* I've seen and personally have experienced is "lack of planning ahead" and "lack of making enough calls".

1. It takes time and effort to plan, especially when you're "on your own" and have to do it yourself.
2. It's easy to avoid those "No's" by saying, "I'll try again later, or tomorrow, because today just isn't my day."

Sounds too familiar? Tomorrow never comes; it's always today. Wherever you are, you have as much time as you need to plan. It's easier to plan than not to plan; when you plan, you relieve your mind and can concentrate on doing other things too. Those calls may be there later, but someone else may have gotten there before you. You all know this, these are not secrets or great revelations. This is what's happening and I just want to refresh your thoughts as to how important discipline really is and that you need to address it; it can be a positive influence, instead of a negative weight on your mind.

I'm not giving you fancy formulas as to what to do about disciplining yourself. You're intelligent and know the score.

Just remember what discipline meant to you as a child; was it good for you?

It's still a very important part of the sales person and sales manager life. Study it, analyze it, practice it, do it, take care of it.

While discipline seems like a negative word, it really is an activity which can make your life much happier. If I had one piece of advice to give anyone in life in any job, it would be, get it done now! At least get started. If you have a project, even your child's work in school or packing for a trip, get your poster board a week ahead, get your suitcase out and then do a little each night - get finished before it is due. What a feeling of accomplishment. Never procrastinate! Start right now by disciplining yourself to sit down and spend 15 minutes working on your next two days, then come right back to the next chapter.

MEETING OBJECTIONS

We've all had the flat "No's!", the "I want to think it over", the "too high", the "wait until next time", and all the other stalls where the doors seem almost closed. We know, however, those answers are just different ways to say "I'm not sure", or "I'm not sold", or "I don't understand". We must simply take their lyrics and compose a good, logical rebuttal to create an opening in their minds which could be music to their ears.

There is a system by which you can formulate a rebuttal to answer any objection with which you could be faced.

It will be important for you to know this system and be able to formulate rebuttals to possible objections that will come up in the sale of your product.

First, you must, again, know your product. We discussed this in Chapter III regarding your confidence. You'll never be able to come up with the answers without the knowledge of your product.

Spend some time now writing down four different objections you have faced within the past week. It doesn't matter how silly or irrelevant they sound. Just write them out.

Now, follow the following simple steps and let's see what kind of rebuttal we can formulate using these steps. Well, let me just give you an example to go by that might fit in to most any product. "I'd like to think it over!"

Step 1. Agree with prospect.
Step 2. Make a logical explanation why you agree.
Step 3. Make a positive statement and get a positive response.
Step 4. Close.

All right, let's see how a rebuttal is formulated.

Step 1. I can certainly understand the way you feel, Mrs. Right.
Step 2. Many of my customers have mentioned the same feelings.
Step 3. However, when they see that they could be taking advantage of this product during a trial period, they feel it is certainly better to have it working for them immedi-

ately instead of waiting and I think so, too, don't you?

Step 4. Why don't we have it shipped Thursday or why don't we enroll you now.

See how logical a rebuttal can be if we follow single steps. See how much better sense it makes than trying to develop a rebuttal off the cuff. Work on yours now and try them this week. Practice them first. If they don't work, use the same system and re-construct another type of rebuttal. The important thing is that the system will help you.

Now that you agree that this system is good, may I ask you to move to the next chapter.

LETEOPAAT

Sounds like a sneeze or the name of a cat or is it a code for one of the most helpful tools in the sales and management business?

One of the biggest challenges we have in the sales and management business is being able to make, accept, and implement the achievement of "Big Goals". We seem to look initially at them as big monsters which we'll ease into and eventually hope we have some big sales to overcome the monster. It doesn't have to be that way.

Ask yourself these questions:

1. Do I know what I want and need to accomplish every day to meet the appropriate part of my overall goal for the year? Do you really know? Exactly? Okay what is it? Write it down now.
2. Do I know what my sales people need to do every day to accomplish their appropriate part of their overall goal for the year? Do you really know?

Should you know? Okay what are they? Write them down now.

3. Do I have a plan to meet those daily objectives and be serious about it as a goal? Do you? Have you determined it is worthwhile to reach your overall goal one day at a time?

4. Do I have a plan to monitor my daily goal achievements and activities of my sales people to monitor their progress, or perhaps you can do it weekly?

How did you answer these questions? If you answered "Yes" to most of them you're in the driver's seat to "LETEOPAAT". Thought I'd forgotten that word by now?

We all know the basics of goal setting: Breaking goals into pieces. Well, it's good advice, but a lot of you don't do it because it takes time and dedication to follow your plan - which we fear we won't do - so we just don't start. We think about it, but it's just easier to think about and not do.

The first thing to remember about "LETEOPAAT" is to believe it will help you "get the job done". Make it an important achievement that is needed, wanted, will be helpful, and is a tool for managing you or others. It will also show you what has not been done.

Okay, the real mystery of "LETEOPAAT". It simply stands for:

"Let's Eat That Elephant One Piece At A Time.

LETEOPAAT

Yes! The quota, the goal, the increase, the job can be much more fun, palatable, and easier to achieve if we achieve one piece of it every day. One piece is easier.

Example:

Goal = 700 unit sales per year
= 14 unit sales per week
= 2.8 unit sales per day
= 1 unit sales per day with 3 sales people

You can see that the daily goal is much less scary, much more believable, and much more achievable.

Rick Pitino, the NBA Coach, had some advice in his book "Success is a Choice". Rick talked about Big Dreams being great, but the long-term successes are a direct result of what you can achieve every day. Long term successes are results of small victories accumulated everyday. What you need to look for are daily successes. It almost sounds too simple.

I have read that Michael Jordan has said that he did not think about getting 32 points in a game. He thought about getting 8 points each quarter.

The teams that play in championship type games are the teams who win more games during the season whether it's daily or weekly.

So "LETEOPAAT". Don't worry if you catch it; it will be helpful to you.

LETEOPAAT to you.

HAVE GRATITUDE FOR YOUR ATTITUDE

"Who cares if you act a fool; the mirror can't talk back to you. Laugh and have a good time, then all bad things will look just fine."

Those are words of a song I used, or wrote to use, during some seminars regarding attitudes. It's not always easy to have a good attitude since there are so many interferences that can draw our minds away from positive directions.

We sometimes question whether we can change from failure or mediocrity to success just by changing our mental attitude. Let's put that question in reverse:

Can we change from success to failure by changing our attitudes? You bet we can. Just start thinking "I can't do this!", "I'll put this off", "I don't want to make that call because no one will be there", "I'll wait to discuss this challenge," and see what happens to your previous success.

1. We could say "That's good enough, we can't do any better" or we could say "That's not good enough - I can do better."
2. We need to give ourselves a chance and don't stop before we get started. Let's dwell on what we can do, not what we can't. Our thoughts must be in changing a day filled with tiresome challenges to a day of interesting opportunities. We must look forward. You can't look forward and backward at the same time.

Our attitude can be our windshield wipers which wipe away the gentle and heavy rains so they do not block our view.

If you feel challenged and not making progress in your job, ask yourself honestly: is the trouble with the job, or is it with your attitude toward your job? It's not easy but we can do something about it. It's okay to be positive; it's okay to express a good attitude openly; it's okay to share your attitude with others. They wish they could have some of your enthusiasm and maybe you can help them develop a better look at their day.

You do not have to do something totally unusual to have a good attitude. Good attitudes are important and should be a part of your normal behavior.

One reason is because of the results different studies have shown. In one study they were determining reasons for successes, promotions. Only fifteen percent of these successes were determined to be caused by education or technical expertise. Attitudes - and the way their work was approached - determined most of these promotions and successes. I am not downing education and technical skills. I am just confirming the importance attitudes play and their necessity for determining successes.

Some people seem to have a good attitude constantly and naturally. Some people seem to always have bad attitudes. The important thing is that we can control them ourselves, even if we have to act like a fool. Who laughed at Robert Fulton, Alexander Bell, and the Wright brothers? We have so many tools to use these days to help us create a good attitude; it's a shame not to use them. Let's list some of the tools.

1. Songs - "You Are the Sunshine Of My Life", "It's Going to Be A Great Day", "Friends", and many, many more!
2. Books - many motivational books, especially this one!
3. Mirrors - Look and laugh; that's easier for some than others.
4. Mouth - Smiling goes so far.
5. Thinking - Our minds can do wonders. Imagine not being able to dream. Imagine letting your

thoughts go wild for a few seconds and what that few seconds can do for a life-time.

There are tools at every turn of our life. We must take advantage of them by looking for the good in everything. Then these tools will jump out and grab you.

Good attitudes create an atmosphere of positive thinking which is simply feeling good even when you feel bad. How can you feel good if you feel bad? It's just a natural phenomenon.

Many books and chapters have been written on attitudes and how they affect our lives. We know what it's all about, don't we. It's just up to us to do something about it.

Get excited, tell someone, and have Gratitude for your Attitude.

OBSTACLES
THEY WILL BE THERE - DEAL
WITH THEM

Obstacles come in many different shapes, forms, ways or whatever you want to call them.

- losing a sale
- losing a good employee
- family challenges
- Personality clashes

Some are obviously worse than others, but most all have things in common.

You feel down, your emotions just run rampant. Our natural instincts kick-in and we start determining how we will "get through" this obstacle or improve this situation.

What's the saying we've heard many times "when one door closes another door opens."

So we must take the attitude that we cannot "wallow" in self-pity too long (even though we must take the appropriate time to adjust according to the obstacle). We must start acting upon the possibilities of overcoming the obstacle. You must make a list of all the ideas you have and actions you can take to overcome your situation, then a light starts shining to show you "the light at the end of the tunnel." Doors open, things start happening, but only when you get active and start looking at the better things to come.

It's not if, but when, obstacles get in your way. You simply must deal with them eventually, then your life will proceed straight ahead.

Just like you'll do with this book. Proceed straight ahead to the next chapter.

LEADERSHIP

General Thoughts That Apply For Leaders

I'll share with you, briefly, some general thoughts on this subject. These will be straight to the point and we'll use bullet points so you can see them clearly.

1. Never tolerate mediocrity
- You set the standard - your success can assure your teams success.
- People must identify with an expectation of a high level of performance.
- Don't expect more than what you are willing to deliver - you can expect similar levels once you have performed.
- Rewards should be granted for results.

2. Don't be satisfied with results too long
- Don't let a good performance make you complacent. Another report will follow quickly.

- If the captain relaxes too long - the crew may go on vacation.
- Build week by week or quarter by quarter to ensure annual needs are met.
- Know that our work is never completely done.
- Leaders should have a vision and be able to see exactly what they want to build or where they want to be.

3. Leaders motivate people by helping them accomplish their own goals. If you help your team members get what they want, you get what you want.

4. Leaders have an attitude.
- An attitude to win.
- Always a positive attitude.
- An attitude of confidence that comes from knowledge.

5. Leaders have a passion to win.
- They are extremely disappointed with losing.
- They have the fundamentals that lead to winning.
- Do not accept or use excuses. Correct what is wrong and move forward.

6. Leaders are dreamers.
- They are always thinking of bigger and higher achievements. Interested in doing things other people are not interested in doing.

Another point we need to know and respect about leaders is they are usually appointed by people below them. Some people may be given titles but, until they are appointed by their team members, they do not automatically become "Leaders." Walking in front of a crowd does not make a leader.

Knowing The Main Objective

One of the primary responsibilities of a leader is to make sure the entire team knows the team's objective. What is the "Main Thing?" Are you sure your team members know the "Main Thing?" You probably would answer yes, but I challenge you to ask them. "Tom, what do you think the main objective is for our team?" You may be surprised that their perception is different than yours.

Let's go one step further: Do you know what the main objective is from your boss? And does your boss know what your main objective is for your team? The point is, we all must be completely clear on our objectives and ensure that everyone does understand them. It is said that when you lose someone who quits their job, they usually quit people, not companies. It could be possible that they never understood the real objective. A good manager or leader should also know his or her employees - especially in a close working relationship - try walking in their shoes!

Get Out of Management Land

Leaders should be out working with their people. There are some team members who take the ball and run hard on their own with very little supervision and guidance. Then the others will usually do as little as they can but not give much at all. You have to be careful not to ignore the super stars nor can you load them up with more work not being done by the others. Don't accommodate the others not doing the work; expectations from everyone need to continue to be at an acceptable level recognizing those doing a great job. By recognizing those people doing the job, you raise the bar for the others.

Leaders Do Things That Are Right

Peoples are constantly watching leaders. So leaders must always do the right things even when no one is watching. If you see something that is wrong, you must not cover it up, turn away or cover your head; you must fix the problem. If you ignore it your team members will notice and you will lose your integrity.

Leaders Have the Right People

People are your greatest asset as a leader. The wrong people provide one of your greatest liabilities.

You must take your time in hiring your team. At times during your interview for hiring people, you may want to allow your team members to help with the interview process. Spending enough time during the hiring of a person can save a lot of time later since you should be able to get better people.

Leaders Control Their Time

Leaders normally do the important things first (list your priorities). Take the unnecessary things off your list. Now be careful not to shuffle and re-shuffle the important things (this can waste time - get the important things done).

We all have meetings. It is important to keep control of them since they can be very time consuming. Make sure you start and end meetings on time. It's not only a time control thing for you; it's a courtesy for the attendees who are trying to control their time. Be very careful not to call meetings without a specific objective to accomplish. Just think if you take 10 people away from their jobs for just 5 minutes, that is 50 minutes of productive time gone.

Leaders Educate Themselves

1. Reading Books
2. Listening to your people (probably the Most Important way to learn)

3. Give of yourself (Be there for your team: give of your time, your experience, your knowledge)

4. Want for their success; help them prepare to "climb that ladder."

And Leaders "Stay Positive - And - Never Give Up"

Every manager has their own style. Mine was a method of surrounding myself with a team who was consistent and persistent; the goal being "we are the best in getting the job done!" I found you have to have a system of accountability - both from you and your people. Remember when establishing your "style", be respectful while you are finding ways that make people tick.

I had been very fortunate to work 31 years for an insurance company called AFLAC. I know you will recognize the name through their great commercials. Dan Amos, CEO and Chairman of the Board, has led AFLAC to become one of the most recognized and successful companies in the world today (a Fortune 500 Company). He possesses all the leadership qualities we have discussed in this chapter. His strong vision, focus, determination, persistency, pride, honesty, visibility and sense of humor have brought out the best in the AFLAC team.

So you can see that these traits and characteristics go along with great leadership.

There will be more tips on "Leadership" mentioned throughout the book, so you have to read on and "Lead the way!"

PLANNING & PREPARATION

To me, one of the key elements of success - whether you are a salesperson or a manager (leader) of some kind - is "Planning" or "Preparation." You can call it anything you want, but I just call it plain ole "Planning."

Tell me: why do people plan weddings? Why do people plan vacations? My guess is that they want to get the desired results. Does that sound reasonable? So they plan each and every detail out to make that adventure successful. Key word is "PLANNING" makes them successful.

I have been amazed throughout my selling and managing career at the number of sales people and managers who have not been taught to or do not actively "plan" for their success.

If you are a sales person, do you make a plan every day to guide you toward your goals? Even if you are in retail sales, hopefully you go to work with a "PLAN" of what you want to achieve that day: replace stock, promote a particular product, determine what items need promotion and give that attention. For outside sales people, you must have each day planned: where are you going, how do you get there, how many sales does it take per day to reach your goals, how many calls, how many referrals.

If you are a manager, you must plan your days also; how many sales in your area do you need to reach your goal, how many sales people need to be involved, how many meetings this week, how many reviews and where. These things just can't be in your mind; they need to be written down somewhere. A day timer or computer is sometimes used - your handheld computer can help you calendar your activities, or the plain ole spiral bound notebook for the less technical people. The form you use will depend upon your type of business. The important thing is to "PLAN" "IN WRITING" what you need to do to accomplish your goals for the day and / or week.

"Planning" sounds simple. Do not underestimate its importance.

"Preparation" is another word sometimes substituted for "Planning." It has a valid right to be a part of planning since preparation can make your plan go more smoothly. For instance, if practicing is part of your overall plan to win a sports game, you must prepare. Preparation would include:

1. Getting the right size shoe to eliminate down-time from blisters.
2. Making sure the socks properly fit and are of correct material to furnish ease of movement and eliminate blisters.
3. In general, you prepare for everything affecting your performance so you can perform at your optimum.

Think about how preparation plays a part in your planning. Again, do not underestimate its importance.

As part of formulating your plan, ideas will "pop-up" all of a sudden that you may be able to place in your plan. Always keep a notebook, computer, or some writing instrument handy to write down your ideas immediately. It's easy to forget them with so much to do these days. These "pop-up" ideas can be very valuable.

Now we will continue on to learn more about leadership in the next chapter.

BEING A WINNER

People have written entire books on this subject but I will try to narrow it down to one short chapter since I know your time is valuable and this book is about getting right to the point.

I've been around winners for a long time and know what it takes to be a winner. I have worked for winners and have managed winners. Here are some traits winners have in common. Take a review of yourself and see how you stack up. Since you are already reading this book, I would bet you have many, if not all of these traits.

Winners

1. Desire to win - they do the things needed to be done to win. They are interested in having more wins than loses. Their desire is much stronger than their abilities. They also want to compete and they hate to lose.

2. Have influence and there is power in their influence. Winners are admired and therefore closely

watched. They have to watch their words since everyone is paying attention. They realize their power to influence others and are careful to use the power appropriately.

3. Have character. Winners are honest with total integrity. There is no gray area here: you either have it or you don't. And winners have it. They have character, honesty, and integrity combined with humility and courage. Sound familiar?

4. Have Focus. Winners have the ability to block out distractions and allow nothing to interrupt their plans. Their focus is on achieving and reaching today's objectives. What you do today is your investment in tomorrow. The game we play today is the most important game. We must win today's game.

5. Have perseverance. Do not let setbacks get to you. A lot of famous people failed many times but did not let the failure get to them. They were stubborn and kept their thoughts on their purpose. We've all heard the words "Stick to it". Three powerful words. Persistence and perseverance have allowed normal people to become great people. There is another saying we are all familiar with which also describes perseverance: "Never give up!" Think about when you have had to "stick to it," to not give up, and had a positive result from it.

6. Have a passion for what they are doing. You need to love what you do. If not, you can have a difficult time winning. There must be energy and enthusiasm for reaching the end result. Winners work hard to make things even better and to take things to the next level.

7. Use time properly. There is simply too much to do. You must have plans and be organized.

8. Don't fake it. You either know it or you don't. This fast moving technological era we are living in will not allow us to fake too much. There is too much accessibility to information.

9. Inspect what they expect. We have to monitor ourselves and/or our team regularly or time will pass and we will lose control.

10. Don't get too comfortable. We cannot let up when everything is going well. Whether you are a sales person or manger, winners stay focused on future goals and do not rest on past successes.

11. Think Big. Winners usually do not think of small accomplishments. Winning means going the extra mile, reaching the higher peak. They dream BIG.

12. Don't cling to the past. If it was not good, get rid of it. If it was good, be glad, but don't dwell too long.

13. Step out of their comfort zone. They do the things never done before. They are interested in big accomplishments to set them apart.

14. Believe in teamwork. We cannot do it alone. Even individual sales people have family, friends, and fellow sales people who help them achieve their goals.

I hope these bullets points about the traits of winners will be helpful to you. My hope is that this entire book is about winners in some way since all the information contained in these pages are to help you become better sales people and/or managers and leaders.

Appearance

Another important part of being or becoming a winner is in the way you present yourself to others. Others can accept you or reject you within the first 30 seconds you meet. Even when others know you already, your appearance will affect the way they react to you. Your appearance simply makes a lasting impression so you want it to be a good one.

Let's talk about how the way you dress and how your body language can help you. I'll put these in outline form so you can see it easily.

1. Clothes must be clean and pressed. I've seen so many people with nice clothes but un-pressed which gave the appearance of "I don't care what people think of me," or it gives the impression that you don't care how you look.

2. Wear clothes appropriate for the event. No jeans at a formal gathering. Most meetings or events give directions on how to dress. When meeting with your boss or clients, look your best and dress up instead of down - unless the occasion dictates a more casual style.

3. Keep your hair neat and in a professional looking style. The grooming of your hair can send both positive and negative signals.

4. There may be differences in acceptance of style depending upon where you live.

5. Make sure to read a book on how to dress successfully.

6. Smile a lot and make sure your teeth look acceptable. While we all may not be able to have perfect teeth, the appearance of crooked and discolored teeth can be a turn off.

7. Look in the mirror before you leave home and make sure everything is in place.

8. Choose someone you think dresses appropriately and try to emulate them.

9. Stand up straight with shoulders back. Posture sends all kinds of signals both good and bad.

10. Don't slump when sitting in a chair.

11. Give space to others. Don't stand close to their face when talking.

12. Be careful of too much hand movement while talking. It can be a distraction.

These are just some basic tips on appearance. Make sure you read a book on how to dress appropriately and discuss the subject with someone you trust and who is a good example.

Appearance is very important. Do not underestimate its effect.

Managers need to be able to advise their team members on proper dress attire when needed. You want your team to have every advantage possible and, again, the first 30 seconds during a meeting can have a big effect on the outcome of the meeting.

STAY IN CONDITION

Part of the overall package of winning is keeping in good condition. You should be aware of your health as far as eating the right foods, keeping your energy level high, and improving your stamina so you are capable of doing your job to the fullest.

There are various exercise opportunities whether you are at home or traveling. You just need to do what is necessary to be where you want to be in the conditioning area. You always want to feel your best in every way. There are great gyms in all towns for men and women.

Let's move forward to the next chapter to find out more tips to help you in your winning ways. So let's get pumped up.

GOALS

Every sales and management book has to have a separate chapter on goal setting.

Ten years from now you will surely arrive, but where? That's a pretty interesting statement / question. If we will arrive and, hopefully, we will arrive somewhere ten years from now, will it be where we want it to be? It can be, but we must plan the trip (there's that word "Plan" again), and we must set the goals of where we want to be. The important thing about setting your goals is that you are deciding where you want to be and you can finally "Plan" how to get there. Then the more exciting realization is that "What you become" by meeting your goals is more important than meeting your goals. Remember, the goals you set (the big ones for sure) must be a journey not a life transformation in 24 hours.

Here are some simple tips concerning goals:

1. Don't make unrealistic goals (Example: lose 100 pounds in one month). If you find them unrealistic, adjust them.
2. Don't set goals too low. We must keep pushing ourselves. We don't want to play in half the game. We want to play the whole game and win.
3. Don't give up because it's hard. You must remind yourself that the end result of achieving your goal is worthwhile. If it were easy, everyone would do it, there would be a store selling it, or there would be a pill for it. Keep your eye on what you want to become and the end will be worth the means.
4. Keep you vision by keeping your discipline of creating and achieving daily goals. "LETEOPAAT."

You get the message without spending more time reading more about goals. Just set them - plan for reaching them - stay disciplined - don't give up - and do it daily.

Now, the short-term goal should be to turn this page and move on to more ideas to put to work.

COMMUNICATING

This is an important subject. How many times have problems come about through a lack of communication or misunderstandings? It has always been amazing to me when there was a miscommunication and after researching the situation, we found there was simply a break down in communication, both written and verbal.

If you cannot communicate with your team, or if you cannot communicate your product to your customers, you can take your philosophies, strategies, and products and toss them in the nearest trashcan.

One of the most important parts of communicating (maybe the most important part) is LISTENING. Listening allows others to feel their thoughts are important. Listening helps you build relationships with people instead of just performing for them. We should be listening four times more than we are speaking. Communication is a two-way street; there should be no winners or losers. Communication should help everyone reach goals.

Ok, now some bullet points on communicating.

1. Reinforce good performance. Whether you are the boss, teacher, parent, or coach, people need to hear you communicate their good performance.

2. Pick up the phone. Talk. Communicate. So many problems deal with "He said this and she said that." Around and around it goes; that's not good. Talk face to face if possible with all parties involved.

3. Put it in writing. Now some things don't need to be written. If you are mad or upset, put off writing to someone until 24 hours have passed and you can think clearly. My suggestion of putting things in writing deals with communicating messages which can be misunderstood through verbal communication. I like to talk to people verbally, then follow up "What you said" in writing so there can be no misunderstandings.

I think you get the point. We must all talk to each other with the thinking of being able to listen more than we talk. We can make others feel good, solve some situations, give our message, and let everyone win.

COMMITMENT

The events of September 11 certainly were absolutely terrifying and sad. The loss of lives and emotional disturbances were unbelievable.

But rushing out of that event came the spirit of America which said, "We are committed", "We are a team", "Nothing can beat us as a team - United." It was great to see people hugging each other, showing love and compassion for their fellow person.

The commitment of overcoming this adversity came through loud and clear. The firemen and policemen were committed to "going all the way." They were COMMITTED.

This type of commitment can help us in reaching our goals. Are we willing to "not be beat" - are we "committed to our goals" - are we willing to "go all the way?"

To break boards in karate you have to commit to believing they will break or you'll hurt yourself. Part of it deals with thinking and believing they will break and being committed to the task. Remember when you tried to break a pencil with one finger, and you did. Then remember when you could not?

Runners go through phases of running depending on how committed they are; do they run long enough to get that second wind, or quit before they "Go all the way." Whatever we do as individuals or teams depends upon what we are:

- Willing to do and
- The commitment we have and
- The belief we have and
- If we are willing to "Go all the way"

Commitment is a choice you need to make in the beginning moments of planning for your success. Do you believe "There are no limits?" Are you willing to "Go all the way?" We have the opportunities. We have to make the commitment.

MEETINGS

I've heard several people tell me something like this: "I don't want to drive 100 miles to our meetings just to have the manager hand out leads. They can send those via email or mail." There is something very wrong with the meeting when people say things like that.

It is the responsibility of the manager (Leader) to formulate a meeting that people want to attend and feel like they will get something worthwhile to help them make their goals.

Meetings are terrific communication tools and can be very effective since you have a team together; they can feed off each other, learn from each other, and create a positive aura for the meeting. But, you must do your part and provide a meaningful, organized agenda that will feed them.

Following is an agenda I used for years. There is nothing fancy about it, just a simple outline to help you get started. If you will look at each section and "fill in" the details, you can have an effective meeting. Take a look.

SUGGESTED OUTLINE FOR MEETINGS

I. Introductions
II. Inspirational
III. Educational
IV. Promotional
V. Motivational

SUGGESTED OUTLINE

I. Introductions

  A. Introduce any special guests at the meeting such as headquarters people or special guest speakers.

  B. Introduce and welcome any new team members.

  C. Set the tone for the meeting by revealing the subject which will be emphasized during the meeting and what you hope to accomplish.

  D. Give short report of your team stats.

II. Inspirational

  A. Good News

    1. Recognize top sales people or achievers

    2. Give any special news for new people

    3. Any other good news

  B. Award winners with appropriate plaques or prizes

C. Use any tapes that are inspirational or possibly a personal word from one of the team members about any experience which could be helpful and inspirational.

III. Educational

  A. Extension of all training subjects.

    1. Sales Presentation (Production knowledge).

    2. Rebuttals: i.e., "No, I have too much" or "I would like to think it over."

    3. Closing (Punch close and Assumptive close).

    4. Get in the door. (First 30 seconds are important).

    5. Referrals. (Always, every time, a must).

  B. Administrative Functions

    1. Filling out forms

    2. Other administrative functions which need further explanations.

  C. Have participation in all educational subjects.

    1. Use role play situations

    2. Encourage discussions, critiques and new ideas.

    3. Plan ahead and let team members perform these role play situations after prior planning on the subject. This will help make it effective and more enjoyable to the others.

Promotional

  A. Promote contests.

  B. Promote trips.

C. Go over the requirements of any contests being promoted.

D. Use charts in the meeting to show the status of the different contests and use individual charts on separate pages to show where each team member stands for each contest.

- Announce any requirement(s) for that particular week for anyone who could win a contest or prize.
- Get all figures each week before the meeting to make everyone aware of where they stand in the different incentives.

Motivational

E. Announce any new incentives or contests for the week, month.

F. Use motivational statements or quotas and discuss motivational literature for reading.

G. Confirm goals for the week, month.

H. Get commitments

I. Help set personal goals for the team members and have them put it in writing for you.

Prior to Meeting, have firm plans for balance of day.

J. Have day of training planned in advance.

K. Have appointments or referrals set up to call on after meeting with one of the team members.

L. Always plan sales activities after the meeting with one of your team members for that day and for the week.

You have an outline on page 100. It's so simple, it will be easy not to use. Please, follow the outline and give it a try. I think you will be satisfied.

NAME TAGS

One last suggestion regarding meetings; I feel "name tags" are very beneficial at meetings - even when you know each other. The name tags lend a professional touch and can create conversation with others you may see throughout the day.

Name tags should be used when there will be 15 or more people at the meeting, or, where the meeting will be filled with people who do not know each other. The "stick-on" tags are sufficient for most meetings when there are cost considerations, but having the metal or heavy plastic ones (with magnetic backing) really look great and are ones you can use over and over.

Along with the name tags, you may want to use "name tent cards" in front of each individual. This allows speakers to be able to call names throughout the presentation.

HAVE SOME GREAT MEETINGS!

I. INTRODUCTIONS

_____

_____

II. INSPIRATIONAL

_____

_____

III. EDUCATIONAL

_____

_____

IV. PROMOTIONAL

_____

_____

V. MOTIVATIONAL

_____

_____

Make copies of this form and use it each time you have a meeting.

IMPROVEMENT

We all want to improve our performance. Sometimes we just need to take a close look and study the situation in order to know how to improve things. Take a look at this brief chapter which gives you some questions to answer so you can determine exactly what you need to do to improve a particular situation or if you even need to improve the situation.

What are some of the things I would need to think about to improve

_____in

(Subject)

my_____?

(Area)

Answer these questions about that subject:

1. Why do you need this item? What benefits would come from doing this?

2. What are the obstacles facing you that are keeping you from doing this?

3. It is possible to do this?

4. Are there ways to climb over or through these obstacles?

5. How much time do you spend each week trying to do this?

6. Is it a matter of finding the time to do this?

7. If so, what is causing you not to have the time?

8. If you prioritized the things you do, where would this item fall as far as importance?

9. When is the last time you attempted this item?

10. How do you propose to change to accommodate this important item?

11. Will accomplishing this item have a direct impact on your life, your team, your financial needs, your team's financial needs?

Tackling tough situations sometimes just means taking a thorough look at how you are approaching it.

We usually can do what we set our minds to do.

BUILDING SELF-ESTEEM

You need to have self-esteem as an individual sales person and you need to not only have it as a manager, but know how to get your team member's self-esteem where it needs to be for them to achieve victories.

When people have self-esteem, they feel good about themselves. How do you get self-esteem as an individual?

You have to look in the mirror. Does he or she work hard enough? Is he/she organized? Does that person look professional? You can't fool the person in the mirror.

So to gain your own self-esteem, you must answer those questions and begin to correct whatever is necessary. The better you do with yourself, the more you build your self-esteem. If you are under-achieving, it's easy to get discouraged and lose your self-esteem.

And remember, it's never too late to change. Change is an absolute must in the world today. We must embrace it and make it fit within our goals. Otherwise we would be fighting a losing battle.

You have to convince yourself before you can convince others.

Plan your approach on your goals, become organized, build discipline to move forward and stay on track, then you are prepared to win and can feel the self-esteem you desire.

You managers need to help your team members build self-esteem. Review their skills with them; be positive about their good skills and make them a big thing, then you can suggest the improvements they need to make to become better and to be at their top. Point out ways for them to improve specifically and urge them to work hard to accomplish these changes.

As a leader, you must know your team members in order to help them. What are their goals? The more you know about them the better you can find the buttons to turn them in the right direction. Knowing all about them shows you care. You need to help them see their value and role.

Always give a positive reinforcement of your team's efforts.

You are in control of your self-esteem. Work hard and you will earn it. You are important, and your contribution is valuable to whatever team you play for.

Now, since you feel good about yourself, let's turn the page and continue on our journey for a few more minutes.

TEAMWORK

You have all heard the slogan!

Together
Each
Accomplishes
More

The word TEAM spells out this slogan appropriately and is completely correct. I heard another slogan a few years ago which I think is great: "Teamwork makes dreams work." Wow, that sounds great.

So let's talk about teamwork. I think one of the best ways to point out its importance is the role it plays in sports. Look at football; there are eleven positions on the field whether they are offense or defense. Each individual has assignments of what to do when the play is called. If everyone doesn't execute their assignment properly, the play will not be successful. If you have a team, every team member should have and know their assignment (what they want to accomplish or the part they play in reaching the teams overall goals). If one team member does not accomplish their assignment, the team may not win. I know all this sounds simple so far and it is. I guess the important part is in getting every team member to know what is expected and how to do it.

Communication is a key factor. We've discussed this in a previous chapter but let's reiterate its importance.

1. The team must have a clear understanding of the team goals.
2. Each member should know exactly what the end result should be.
3. Each team member should understand what their role is and work with the leader on "Plans" (there's that word again) on how to achieve success regarding their assignment. This may take practice, organization, discipline. But everyone must be distinctively clear of the part they play.

Now the team knows the goal, and you, as the leader, must develop a plan for the team to succeed. The word "Plan" keeps coming up on a regular basis.

We all know games aren't really won on the day of the game. It's the days of practice and rehearsal that prepares the individuals to work as a team on game day. The game day performance is a result of the preparation and practice prior to the game.

Your success as a sales person, or manager, depends upon your discipline to plan, practice, and execute. When each individual can plan, practice, and execute their assignment, teamwork is in its finest place and the chance of winning is most probable.

Leaders must read, read, read, read, read about everything, then you can converse with others about things going on in the world. Knowledge is Power and you can certainly gain that power and knowledge by reading.

Remembering Names

Leaders make it a practice of remembering people's names. There's nothing that sounds better to them than their own name and to know you have remembered their name. It means that they are important to you. Try to associate their name with something familiar. With the name Mary Woods, you could be visualizing a happy girl, named Mary, running through the woods.

So remember, when we help each other everyone accomplishes more. The key is communication of the goal, planning the activity to reach the goal, disciplining the team to practice and rehearse, then execute on game day.

IN SUMMARY

I have not separated selling from managing in this book because whether you are a sales person or a manager, you need to be aware of all these tips. Sales people have an opportunity to become managers and managers need to be aware of tips for their sales people.

So I hope this book was enjoyable to you, made you aware of some things to improve, and gave you some tips to make your job be more effective.

You took the "TIME" to read this book and find some "Tips on being organized". Organization can give you "Confidence" in selling "What you really want to sell". Now you can "BIP" your goals after "setting your goals," and "PLAN" how to reach them. Today is the day important to you; don't pass it up. Use your telephone conversations to help you get the appointment and be persistent when needed. You must stay disciplined. You have your vision and make sure you "LETEOPAAT" your way to success. Make sure your attitude is right as you deal with the objections you face each day so you can make the decisions on how to get that sale.

As you see success happening to you and you take the action to head in that direction, obstacles will get in your way. But you have learned to face these obstacles through planning and preparation, through your commitment to being a winner, and you have learned a lot of leadership traits which will keep you inspired.

Remember to have effective meetings, and communicate well with your team. Establish your style!"

We have covered a lot of Tips all in this summary. Now go back and select the ones you want to work on now; re-read the chapter and practice, practice, practice.

Most of all, believe in you. Your vision, your motivation, and your will to succeed will carry you far in life. Believe in hard work and believe in trying; that's the first step.

Thanks for joining me in this journey. Again, the joy we get is in the trip toward our goals when we are having fun accomplishing some part of the goal every day.

Now, GO FOR IT!

Jim Thompson has worked in different sales and management positions for forty-five years. He has sold anything from ladies and men's shoes to chemical products, industrial packaging supplies, and insurance. For thirty-one years he was employed by AFLAC in various positions, which promoted the sales of their products. Jim helped develop new areas such as the Broker market place for insurance sales and led AFLAC's largest sales territory to the number one position in total sales from 1995 through 2005. Jim had the opportunity to work with many of the top leaders in the AFLAC field force who were the number one sales team in their area. The tips and information in the book is what he learned and what he taught and promoted to sales people. These ideas and tips have already passed the test. After reading so many books on sales and management, Jim wanted to share his thoughts and ideas in a way that allows people to be able to get the message quickly and be able to get the information working quickly. Jim hopes you enjoy and learn from these tips. Jim is married to Pat, has two daughters, and five grandchildren.

TATE PUBLISHING & *Enterprises*

Tate Publishing is committed to excellence in the publishing industry. Our staff of highly trained professionals, including editors, graphic designers, and marketing personnel, work together to produce the very finest books available. The company reflects the philosophy established by the founders, based on Psalms 68:11,

"THE LORD GAVE THE WORD AND GREAT WAS THE COMPANY OF THOSE WHO PUBLISHED IT."

If you would like further information, please call
1.888.361.9473
or visit our website
www.tatepublishing.com

TATE PUBLISHING & *Enterprises*, LLC
127 E. Trade Center Terrace
Mustang, Oklahoma 73064 USA

STEVEN TALC

Level Up

HOW TO BECOME A GREAT
PROFESSIONAL SOFTWARE DEVELOPER

Level Up!

How to Become a Great Professional Software Developer

Steven Talcott Smith

This book is for sale at http://leanpub.com/level_up

This version was published on 2014-11-15

Leanpub

This is a Leanpub book. Leanpub empowers authors and publishers with the Lean Publishing process. Lean Publishing is the act of publishing an in-progress ebook using lightweight tools and many iterations to get reader feedback, pivot until you have the right book and build traction once you do.

Tweet This Book!

Please help Steven Talcott Smith by spreading the word about this book on Twitter!

The suggested hashtag for this book is #secretsoftheaelogicians.

Find out what other people are saying about the book by clicking on this link to search for this hashtag on Twitter:

https://twitter.com/search?q=#secretsoftheaelogicians

This book is a waypoint on a journey I started long ago. I do not yet know where it will lead. I have many people to thank for inspiring me, for teaching me, for encouraging me. The person I want to thank most of all is my wife, Celda. Thank you for your Love and support. Thank you for not being too hard on me when I am present in body but my mind is elsewhere, thinking about software, business or writing.

I want to thank our staff in the Philippines, in particular, Nestor Pestelos for reading and reviewing drafts and for taking an interest in this project.

Contents

CONTENTS

CONTENTS

Introduction

This book is a simple guide to help you in your career advancement as a professional software developer.

Audience

I wrote the first edition of this book as a guide for the current and future employees of my firm, ÆLOGICA. I have since expanded and adapted the content to serve anyone pursuing a career as a software developer.

The content is primarily aimed at those who are in the first 5 or 10 years of their professional career and those who find themselves responsible for managing such people.

In order to have a lasting and successful career as a professional developer, you should strive to achieve above-average results. While innate skills have a major role to play, this book aims to describe the habits, attitudes, and perspectives you should cultivate in order to consistently perform at your best.

I wrote this book for the ambitious developers – the ones who want to make the most of themselves and their career – the ones who want to Level Up!

How to Read Level Up!

It is possible and not too strenuous to read this book in a single sitting. I know – I have re-read it several times this way. At its present size, it should take about 90 minutes to at most 2 hours. If you do not have this much time, try to read the first two chapters and then dive into any chapters that particularly interest you.

What is Software Development?

Software is the form or channel by which human will or intent enters and controls the computer. Our task as software developers is to make something concrete and useful out of the infinite and abstract possiblities afforded by computation. We help users to use their computers or devices to accomplish their specific tasks and objectives.

The technology and methods by which we accomplish this undergo constant change. Success involves acquiring competency in multiple technical disciplines.

Professional Software Development

Software development as a profession is still only a couple of generations old in the developed world. In many developing countries it is still newer. While humans have undertaken to develop software for more than 50 years, commercial opportunities for software outside of large institutions only arrived with the advent of Microsoft and the invention of the personal computer in the 1980s. The growth of the commercial Internet in the late 1990s and early 2000s multiplied opportunities for developers and also opened the profession to global competition. The success of smartphones and tablets as platforms for apps and mobile websites have only continued this trend.

Professional software development is different from software development undertaken by the hobbyist, the student, the amateur, or even the technical-entrepreneur. Many people learn to program and to develop software in the course of pursuing some other aim. Professional software developers build software for others as a career. Clients often pay professional fees to the developer or their employer for their work. At the very least your employer is paying you a salary for your professional expertise and skill.

Professional software development is usually a "team sport". Done right, it requires good communication, collaboration, imagination, and an understanding of how users approach computers as well as the broader context in which our creations are used.

Ageism in various parts of the industry may reduce the visibility of older developers but they are out there. Although not necessarily as visible to those early in their careers, many more experienced developers enjoy fruitful and rewarding careers into middle age and beyond. It behooves anyone contemplating a long career in this field to understand how to acheive longevity. Outside of the developed world however, such senior role models are hard to find.

The demands and competitive nature of software development tends to discourage those who are not both highly skilled and dedicated to their craft. When you meet someone older who is doing active development, seek to learn what you can from them as they likely possess valuable knowledge and perspectives that your younger peers do not.

Successful career longevity requires the cultivation of certain attitudes, abilities, and approaches most of which are embodied in our notion of a professional developer.

Craft vs *Profession*

My colleague, Obie Fernandez, author of the The Rails Way and serial entrepreneur, once described software development as a "post-industrial craft." His apt description encapsulated some key insights that helped inform my understanding of this thing that we do. Craftsmanship is clearly an essential aspect of our work and the craft perspective permeates parts of the professional press with such titles as "Apprenticeship Patterns" and "The Pragmatic Programmer".

Craftsmanship evokes passion, aesthetic concerns, and an apprenticeship training model which fits practical software development well.

In addition to the craft terminology, we also use a different word with equally important associations: **Profession**. I use this because professionalism entails notions such as *professional responsibility* as well as an identity with your career, network, and peer-group that transcends your employer or employers.

Analogies and distinctions may be made or drawn with other professions such as Law, Medicine or Accounting. I do not subscribe to the idea that licensure or regulation are required to make one a "professional software developer". It has more to do with how you perform the development and in what capacity. Certainly as a career, it can be as rewarding or demanding as other traditional fields.

Logic and Beauty in Software Development

Logic is the process of reasoning according to strict principles. It can be deductive (abstract to concrete) or inductive (concrete to abstract). We apply both kinds of reasoning in our work. As all developers know, computers adhere very strictly to logical rules. One cannot hope to become an effective software developer without having or developing a strong and swift logical mind.

Aesthetics deals with principles of beauty and questions of artistic judgement. Those lacking in good judgement cannot discern whether one thing is better than another.

We seek to create value for our customers and the users of our software. Value requires good judgement.

The judgement of a software developer, particularly the experienced full-stack developer, ranges over the gamut of technical, architectural, and user experience concerns. We do not expect someone else to make our creations easy to use and attractive after we are done. Nor do we abdicate responsibility for the final product to a design we receive like a set of stone tablets. If we detect problems or can suggest improvements, we say something.

In many environments, we are often the last stop on the production line before code ships to users. Formal quality assurance (QA), when it is a factor at all, may not question the user experience or design. Often it is up to us in small ways to make continual improvements not merely in our code or architecture, but also in the product *as it is experienced by the end user.*

In short, we care not only how to make it work, but also how it *should work* for the user and how it *should work* under the covers. This is craftsmanship.

> We named our company "ÆLOGICA" because it is a made-up word which evokes or represents the combination of *aesthetics* and *logic* that we bring to our craft as software developers.

Deliver Value

We seek to deliver value every day. Individually, as a team, as a company, and over the course of our careers, we want to **maximise our pace of value creation and delivery**.

In an increasingly frictionless world, the best work and the best projects go to the best teams, wherever they are. The best teams are those that consistently create the most value in the least time. Being at or near the top has a compounding effect over the course of your career.

> Relentless focus on value production will ensure that you enjoy the best your chosen career has to offer for as long as you wish.

Subjectivity of Value

Value is subjective – it is attributed to something by *someone*. Therefore we must consider who does the valuing. We must try to understand what they value about our work and why. Three important parties attribute value to our creations:

1. The User
2. The Owner
3. The Developer

We always try to put the User first. However, the Owner pays the bills. Usually what is in the best interest of the User is also best for the Owner.

> When the values of the User and the Owner conflict, many of the best developers feel something of a dilemma or ethical challenge. We want to avoid this. If you feel this is happening, speak up – others may share your concern.

Owners typically recognize one of two modes of value: making money or saving money.

What the Developer values often can be understood or reinterpreted more usefully in terms of value to the Owner or the User. As an exercise, the developer should learn to restate his or her values in terms of value to others. If neither the User nor the Owner value a particular thing its value may be discounted or disregarded for practical purposes.

For example, let us say that the Developer values a clean, consistent architecture in the code. This same thing may provide the Owner with strategic options, delayed obsolescence, a more reliable team, lower downtime, fewer errors, etc. It may yield a lower total cost of ownership and higher customer satisfaction. (lower costs, makes more money)

Likewise, let us imagine a developer values small commits consisting only of related changes. For a system owner this might mean faster troubleshooting and lower downtime when an issue is discovered in production. (lower costs, makes more money) It might also make it easier to identify under-performing team members. (lower costs)

 Learn to re-state your values in the language of others.

Connecting to the Value

Users use computers very differently than programmers. They may not even know they are using software or not know whose software they are using. They may know only the task they wish to accomplish and sometimes even that may seem vague to them.

Many developers are surprised and frustrated to learn just how normal people interact with their machines.

As professional developers, we do not view users with contempt or indifference. We seek to empathise with them.

A user typically uses software to accomplish a task in order to achieve some value. For example, a user may be concerned with pleasing the boss, communicating with a coworker as part of their job, shopping for a needed item, organising their day, fulfilling administrative duties ("paperwork"), researching a problem, engaging in training, assessing their financial status, accessing entertainment, communicating with a friend, attracting a mate or getting a date.

Whatever the users are doing they generally do not think of themselves as using software. The value of the software to the end user is how quickly, efficiently, and perhaps even pleasantly it allows them to accomplish their personal or professional tasks.

The Owner of a software system typically is concerned with how the software functions or will function in support of business or organisational objectives. Primarily, these objectives consist of making money or saving money. In general, one must make money before one can save it. Therefore one typically prefers to focus effort on development aimed at making money. Saving money is good, it is merely of secondary importance to making more money.

Specific concerns may typically be classified under the headings of making or saving:

- Are users adopting it? (Are we going to *make* money?)
- Is it cost-effective? (Am I going to *save*?)
- Are the users buying, clicking-through, transacting, using or otherwise doing whatever I want them to do with the software? (Are we *making* money?)
- If not, why not? (Why aren't we *making* money?)
- Does the software expose us to risk? (Am I going to *lose* money?)
- What kind and how much? (Exactly how and how much am I going to *lose*?)
- Will the software asset produce the expected Return on Investment? (Are we going to *make* money?)
- Will the returns exceed the opportunity cost? (Should I be doing something else to *make more* money?)

These are typical concerns of the Owner.

When the owner of a system is a corporation or institution of more than one person, value to the owner must be distinguished from value to the owner's agents or employees. Herein lies the troubling domain of politics.

> On Politics
>
> As much as possible, we professional developers wish to concentrate responsibility for decisions related to what gets developed into a single individual in order to shield ourselves from the distraction of organisational politics. This is easier to do across the vendor-client relationship where such things can

> be spelled out contractually. This is one advantage outside developers have over developers employed directly by the owner of a software asset. Within a company, one may strive to report to a single manager responsible for tasking.

Before setting out on any software development task, make sure you are clear on who needs, values, or wants what you are about to do and at least ask yourself why they want it.

If you are unclear about why they might want it, ask the product owner! If you suspect it may lead to an enlightening discussion or if you find the initial answer unsatisfactory, proceed to ask the 5-Whys[1]. However, instead of looking for the root cause of a problem, here we seek to learn the root motivation for a feature.

 Understand the *who* and *why* of any feature or product.

Now that we have connected to the value, how do we apply this to our daily work?

---

[1]http://en.wikipedia.org/wiki/5_Whys

Setting a Value Alarm

Developers often enjoy a great amount of autonomy in their work and so must be responsible for managing their time effectively every minute and every hour. We believe effective time management is one of the key abilities that separate the best developers from the rest. Unlike some abilities or qualities which are harder to change, time management is something we can all improve.

Connecting to the value and managing your time intersect through a process I call the "Value Alarm". If you have had the opportunity to pair program much, you will notice that the better developers in your team already do this instinctually.

Basically, every time you take your break (and you do take breaks don't you?) before you step away (and you do stand up and walk away from the workstation during your breaks, right?), ask yourself or your pair partner:

1. "What have we been doing for the last X minutes?"
2. "Is this creating value for the User or the Owner or not?"

A good pair partner who is playing the navigator role (not driving) will ask this question even more frequently. If you are really disciplined, you might ask every several minutes.

If the answers are, "chasing our tail," and "no, not really", think of it like a "red light." It means stop. It is time to reset and get back on track.

Developers often get caught up in hyper-focus working for the framework or the test rig, doing pointless ceremony or picking at little nits of no particular importance. Time adds up and wasted time adds up quickly. It is easy to blow a quarter of a day on something of low value or importance if you are not careful. Do this regularly and you will be regarded as a low-performing team or developer (or maybe merely average).

Do not confuse low-value work with important work that often must be done to "clean things up" or generally improve project infrastructure. Both of those activities do add value though it may not be easily apparent. It's definitely a "yellow" light situation which indicates caution.

Practice questioning yourself like this several times per day, preferably at least once per hour and you will quickly form an extremely valuable habit.

You will notice that you become more conscious of your own time and you will become increasingly frustrated with aspects of development that waste your time, where we define "wasting time" as performing tasks while "on the clock" that do not create value for the Users or the Owners.

It is quite possible to waste entire days and even weeks. The naive developer may look quite busy and imagine that he or she is performing the job. They are not. Internal developers can get away with this by leaning on compartmentalised knowledge or favouritism for job security when value production is low. Outside professionals cannot.

Automate Your Chores

Always look for ways to automate away "busywork". Time-consuming tasks that do not add a lot of value – activities you think of as "doing it manually" – should be automated wherever possible. Generally if it will take me only a little longer to automate something than it would to do it manually, I will automate. It may take a little longer but at least I have produced something reusable and I didn't get bored or make manual errors.

If it seems likely I will have to do the procedure again, I will certainly automate it. If there is a chance I might screw it up with a type-o or manual error and have to do it over or cause some damage, I will automate.

Software as both Asset and Liability

The more you can understand how the owner of a piece of software values it, the better you can ensure that you are creating value and the more easily you can articulate that value to the people who pay for it.

In Business and Investment, an asset is something that produces Income. An asset costs something to acquire or develop. This is the initial investment, sometimes also thought of as "sunk cost"[2]. In the physical world, assets often require maintenance. Consider a commercial building. It can be rented out to tenants to produce an income, but like any structure, it is degrading due to wear and tear, weather, rust, rot, etc. Competitive structures are built with more modern features and perhaps better adapted to market needs. Furthermore, regulations change and buildings must be retro-fitted.

Clearly, in addition to the initial investment, there is a cost of ownership consisting of maintenance and occasional upgrades.

Software is no different. It requires upkeep. Cutting corners during development can diminish the value of the asset over its lifetime by increasing the cost of ownership. Neglecting to maintain the asset may diminish its value rapidly. In a very competitive market, the ongoing cost of ownership may be similar to the costs experienced during development.

All production software code is both a liability and an asset for the owner. The more code you have, the more expensive it will be to maintain. The value of the asset consists of the difference between the net present value of the total system benefits and the net present value of all system liabilities.

Value is not the same thing as cost. Acquisition cost is always a sunk cost. That is, the acquisition or development

---

[2]http://en.wikipedia.org/wiki/Sunk_cost

cost of a system has no bearing on the current value of the system. A system is not "worth $250,000" because it cost $250,000 to develop. Replication cost is sometimes a factor in valuation but only in the absence of other more useful metrics.

Factors adding value to a software asset:

- Expected probable future income
- Probable market value if sold
- Quantifiable benefit to users
- Adaptability/Enhanceability
- High-speed, disciplined team

Factors which detract from the value of a software asset:

- Present deficiency that will result in wasted or time effort in the future
- Future maintenance costs
- Future infrastructure cost
- Legal, financial, or reputation risk

At a more concrete technical level the following system assets and liabilities may be more familiar to the developer:

Software Assets	Software Liabilities
Clean, Necessary Code*	All Code
Test Suite	Dead Code
Consistent Environments	Poor Test Suite
Well-sized Commits	No CI
Simple branching	Premature Optimization
Security Review	Premature Abstraction
Continuous Integration	Obsolete Comments
Organised Docs & Artefacts	Lost Docs or Design Artefacts
A Smooth Functioning Team	Team Dissolved

Not all owners of software assets understand the liability aspect very well. Confusion regarding this aspect leads to frustration. The developer may not know whether to architect software for the long term or treat everything as a throwaway experiment during "business model or customer discovery." Sometimes it is appropriate to "move fast and break things" while at other times we want to exercise great care, minimize downtime or take time to polish. If the owner undertands these aspects of ownership well, we can make better decisions about which approach to apply.

Whatever business or development philosophy prevails at different points in your career, you will observe nothing is quite so permanent as the "throwaway code" that ends up doing something useful. And nothing is quite so tragic as the lovingly-crafted system representing enormous personal and capital investment that goes nowhere in the market.

 Always attempt to clarify whether the Owner is experimenting or developing for long term sustainability and competitiveness so you can weigh your architectural decisions accordingly. Always know the approximate time budget for the project or the portion that you are working on and use that to inform your choices.

Even if a project is experimental and expected to be thrown away, try to employ best practices and follow conventions whenever time permits. When presented with two options of equal value and effort, *go with the approach that makes future changes easier.* You will inevitably be dealing with the mess later.

Climb the Abstraction Ladder

Big upfront architecture can be difficult to justify on a per-project basis. Ten or fifteen years ago, Design Patterns dominated the current thinking about architecture.

We were supposed to learn to communicate with UML diagrams and sketch our systems in advance with pretty pictures before setting down to code. Pretty much all of that disappeared. I haven't used much UML in years and I have been highly productive.

Today we talk about frameworks. Frameworks and the consensus practices that arise around them take care of many architectural decisions for us.

The genius of a framework like Ruby on Rails is that it captures all of the essential common elements of a whole class of applications (web applications with a single persistent store of data) very well. The adoption among leading developers spurred nearly a decade of open source investment such that Rails itself must have a value in the billions of dollars.

An opinionated framework like Ruby on Rails frees developers from having to reinvent the wheel on each project. It discourages less experienced developers from making big architectural mistakes and allows experienced developers to focus on the finer points of building great applications.

These days there are many good frameworks out there. Some are weaker than others. The framework is a means to an end. The end is producing value for others and happiness for yourself. If you feel too much pain around the framework you are using, look around for other options. If you feel out of touch with the community or your peers who work with a given technology stack, look for something else. If your employer will not consider better technology that will allow you to produce more value and be happier in your work, it may be time to look for another job.

 Always remember that you are a software developer first, not a developer of a specific framework or language. Chances are you will use multiple languages and frameworks, often in the context of a single project. Over the course of your career you can expect to change. That said, become expert in something that is widely used and which you are happy to use so you will enjoy more career options and more satisfying work.

For web applications, Rails and the Ruby community surrounding it continues to advance the state of the art, inspiring many imitators. Will Rails always be at the forefront of web development? Who knows? It is not clear that any of the current contenders can or will unseat it. What we do know is that we constantly want to seek frameworks and languages that remove ceremony, reduce code, and allow us to create value faster. When something comes along that allows us to do that, I will consider using that instead.

Always Deliver

Delivering means shipping. Unshipped features, unmerged work on branches, vague ideas, architectural notes for software that doesn't run yet or squiggles on a whiteboard might as well not exist. When it comes to *Delivering Value*, all that matters is what you have shipped or turned over to the owner and given to the users.

Often delivering value means sacrificing progress on features in the pipeline or backlog to polish and deliver what you already have working. Software can require endless tweaking. There is always more to do and features that could be added. Some features will have someone loudly advocating, "the customers are screaming for this."

The successful professional developer must exercise the discipline and authority to postpone work on new features until in-progress work is delivered.

Often a strong software team can produce faster than a single individual (who may have other responsibilities) can process or consume its output. When this happens, an inventory of undelivered features will accumulate. This represents a bit of a crisis which may have repercussions on velocity and quality for weeks or months.

The burden for resolving this situation may lie with the Owner but the developers (who share responsibility for the overall outcome) need to raise the red flag and ring the alarm when it starts to happen.

Track Your Time

Remember that all value is perceived value. For the professional developer it is incredibly important that the Owner perceive the value. A professional developer whose time is billable always needs to stand ready to justify his or her work and production. Employees may also be wise to keep a good record of how they spend their time if only for self-improvement. Time logs are a key part of the process.

Professional developers typically use some form of time-tracking to track their hours. Time entries are associated with projects and typically contain some written note regarding what was accomplished during the period in question. Naive developers or those unaccustomed to professional work often neglect to say anything meaningful or valuable in these notes such as, "worked on feature X" or they write notes that only they understand by for example, pasting a bunch of poorly summarized and overly technical commit messages.

The best form of time tracking note is something that is understandable and legible to the product owner and clearly speaks to some value delivered. Imagine you are in the position of auditing the time logs of a contracted development organization. What sort of messages would you want to read as you were skimming along? Those are the notes you want to leave in your time tracking system.

Making time log entries at various points or at the end of your day is a great occasion to take stock of what you are doing and how valuable it was or was not.

Example

Let us say you are closing out a time entry of 2.3 hours. You changed a formula in a report, updated tests, handled some merge conflicts due to a team member misusing the version control then successfully got your changes through CI and deployed on staging. You could write each step but that is unnecessary and it makes you seem like you are trying to appear more busy or productive than you were. Instead, put something short, simple and true such as, "delivered new formula for stock valuation report."

Time entries should be either a single line or a short bulleted list of items that are at least meaningful if not obviously valuable to the system owner.

Do not make passive-aggressive log entries or make commit messages that will cast a bad light on your teammates. These things should be addressed directly or during standup, or if necessary escalate them to management.

Takeaways

- Focus on producing value
- Be careful when interests diverge
- Restate your values in the language of others
- Empathize with Users; do not view them with contempt

- Understand the *who* and *why* of every feature
- Set a "Value Alarm" – constantly ask yourself, "is this important?"
- Understand the system as both an asset and a liability
- Your job is to increase the assets and decrease the liabilities
- Always deliver
- Track your time effectively

Craft Quality

"The test of the machine is the satisfaction it gives you. There isn't any other test. If the machine produces tranquility it's right. If it disturbs you it's wrong until either the machine or your mind is changed." - Robert M. Pirsig, Zen and the Art of Motorcycle Maintenance: An Inquiry Into Values

Achieving consistently high quality seems to be one of the greatest challenges of software development. In spite of many books, methodologies and even an entire subfield of Quality Assurance that seek in part to address the issue, poor-quality software is still more of the rule than the exception.

One now traditional trope in software development is that you get to choose only two out of these three values: *good*, *fast*, and *cheap* [^1]: The Iron Stool[3]. In reality, taking longer is likely to drive up the cost and does not in itself guarantee a better result. Spending more does not necessarily make a project or team go faster.

Most will concede that it is possible to make things poorly and quickly. This usually appeals to the buyer or manager

---

[3]http://www.codinghorror.com/blog/2006/10/the-iron-stool.html

for whom cost is the primary concern. A developer or consultant will typically trot out this saying to remind such people that they are about to be handed a pile of garbage, because they supposedly could not afford the time to make it better.

Such simplistic analysis will not serve our purpose here. As professional developers, we aim to achieve a consistently high level of Quality. In order for us to do that we need to understand Quality itself better.

What is Quality?

Quality means different things to different people. A designer may imagine the quality is an aspect of the design or adherence to the design. A programmer might imagine it is a matter of architecture and test coverage and an absence of bugs. QA managers may take a process-oriented view.

It is possible try to impose quantitative measures such as defect rates on a system in order to "measure quality". This approach probably works well for mass manufacturing or for producing items according to very strict specifications but it seems to miss quite a lot of the picture when it comes to software.

These approaches to Quality, while individually valid, fail to capture its essence. Quality is something that is perceived. Like value, it is subjective. The Quality of an item or system can perhaps be best ascertained by asking a question about how one feels when one is using it:

Does it feel like the person or people who made this thing cared?

Did the makers care? Did they care about me, the User? What does that say about the maker? What did they want me to think about them? What did they want their peers to think? What did they think about themselves? Do they care what anyone thinks? Were they trying to be the best? Or was the maker just some schlub flinging something together to please a boss?

The Craftsmanship Approach

The craftsman cares about the users of his or her creations. The craftsman shows pride through workmanship. The craftsman does not need to be told to do a good job – to make it look good, to make it smooth, to clean up the mess underneath, even in the parts nobody is likely to see.

You know you have done a good job on something when you really want to sign your name to it and say, "there – I made *that*!" or when you want to show it to people who may be only marginally interested.

The craftsman wants to do the best job possible within the given constraints. The craftsman will feel discouraged and listless if he or she must compromise too greatly on Quality. This is also sometimes referred to as "passion".

The professional software developer must reconcile passion, craftsmanship, and artistic sensibility with the constraints of budget, ability, and personality. Reconciliation is comprised of hundreds or even thousands of little tradeoffs made during the course of a project. The result is clear in summation.

If the tradeoff was always to do the expedient thing, to never spend time polishing, then the result will be a grotesque monstrosity that is difficult to use and ugly to look at. It will be obvious that no one cared.

Endless polishing to the point of never shipping features, also does not serve the user, much less the owner. We strive for a middle way.

We put Users first in our value hierarchy because that helps us to make the right trade-off decisions.

 You will never go too far wrong by trying to do what you think is best for the User.

In the end the User must judge quality of these artifacts. We build our systems for Users. Users must ultimately find it valuable enough to use and come to love it or hate it. The User suffers if we fail to deliver or if late delivery jeopardizes the entire enterprise.

As professional craftsmen, we recognize that Quality is not someone else's job. Producing quality work is our job and we need to own it, whether or not there is anyone around with "Quality" in their job title.

Polish

Correctness denotes adherence to an explicit design. Since we practice agile, and we are pragmatic, we know that in the real world, designs are often incomplete and almost always require modification. Correctness or accuracy cannot therefore be the sole determinant of Quality. It may not even be very important. We developers are expected to use our brains more. At the very least we should know when to enlist someone more skilled in design to address a problem.

"Polish" is both a verb and a noun. As a noun, it refers to the "fit and finish" of a product. People often mean Polish when they talk about Quality.

Polish consists of things rarely specified explicitly but which will improve the user experience or appearance of the thing produced. Examples of polish may include getting the balance, spacing or color of visual elements just right or adjusting them after real world data alters the original speculative design.

Polish may include getting the keyboard focus right when a page is loaded. It may require understanding the default path or most-common use case and making that especially easy to complete. Polish may consist of removing redundant information that has crept into the user interface or taking other steps to reduce the cognitive load on the user or the time required to complete a task.

Always set aside a reasonable amount of time to polish your work.

One excellent strategy for ensuring that you have time to polish is to focus on development in the morning and polish after lunch. Toward the end of the day, choose features that are comprised of simple UX improvements or look around for things to clean up that may not be listed in the backlog. To do this, you really need to focus on finishing your core development in the morning. This means you need to hit the ground running when you first start. By mid-morning you should already have delivered something. A slow start in the morning will make it impossible to find time to polish later.

Efficiency Impacts Quality

For any given feature, there is a Minimum Essential Effort (MEE) inherent in creating that feature. It is the amount of cognitive effort that is required of the whole team when everything goes "just right." MEE is related to the intelligence and skill of the team members and to the minimum clock time (as distinguished from calendar time) spent on the feature. The MEE is considered to be that spent by the entire team including those requesting or specifying the feature and those who may be involved in implementing it, as well as those who may consume it and validate or accept it.

When one part of the team performs weakly by for example, not exerting enough effort at the right time, additional cognitive effort is required of the other team members and perhaps even of the weak performers later on as work is sent back for revision or extra review. Weak feature descriptions or design will increase the burden on the developers. If the developers are unable to pick up the slack and improve the feature requirements or description, the whole team will chase its tail with rework due to misunderstanding or lack of clarity about what exactly was supposed to be done. Not only does this result in inefficiency, but it leads to quality problems.

When the efficiency of the team is low, Quality suffers. As time runs short, the first thing teams tend to sacrifice is any notional time for "polishing." Often no time is budgeted for polishing and teams just hope to have enough or somehow make it a part of everyday work. A fast team will find surplus time for polishing whether it was explicitly budgeted or not. At fast team will find little wins and ways to leverage small amounts of time for polish that a slow team will let go to waste. An inefficient team will almost never polish their work. It shows.

Teams need to know how much polish is expected of them.

 Establish acceptance policies that include the level of polish. Do not approve or submit features until the desired level of polish is reached.

Quality Features

There are many places where quality problems enter the software development production line. Since user stories or features are the "input" to the software production process, the place we will look for problems is feature definition.

Many problems arise from poorly defined features. If we have garbage going in, we should not be surprised to see garbage coming out. Almost any agile project or team can benefit from enhancing the clarity and quality of the User stories.

Developers often tolerate poorly defined User stories because they do not know how to write them well themselves. They often assume wrongly or naively that others know how to tell them what they want. Even experienced product managers sometimes fail to express themselves clearly enough to developers.

 Always be willing to press your own standard of excellence and to raise the level of quality in the work of those around you.

At ÆLOGICA, we created a model of what a good user story looks like. Developers should not estimate features or stories which do not conform to this model. Instead the developer should take it upon themselves to re-word and improve the feature *before* estimating or starting work on it.

Feature Naming

We start with how a feature is named. Often features appear casually named or phrased in terms of some general capability. When we encounter features worded like chores, we should either convert them into chores or reword them into the proper form. The proper form is:

1   `<role> <verb> <object>`

Examples:

1. admin creates a user
2. editor adds image to email templates
3. evaluator views list of skills in functional area

Strike any phrases such as "has ability to" or modal verb forms (those using "can ...") as these are redundant. Redundancy adds noise when scanning lists such as a list of features in a backlog.

Conveying the right amount of information in the feature name is key. Long feature names with a high degree of specificity crowd out other items and make it difficult to "scan" down a list. Features names may wrap to two lines but if they wrap to three or more they probably should be shortened.

Feature Description: Who, What, Why

We follow a variant of the Gherkin syntax[4] to elaborate essential information about a feature. The opening sentence of the feature must cover three things:

- who will use the feature
- what the user will do
- why user wants to do that

Feature descriptions often neglect to mention who wants the feature or why they want it. This is very important information. When you are busy discussing many features and populating an icebox or backlog, the who and why may seem obvious from the context. Weeks or months later, however, it may not be so clear. The resulting confusion can require you to perform guesswork and to possibly misinterpret aspects of the feature leading to wasted time. You cannot make proper tradeoff decisions without a clear understanding of who is using the feature, what they seek to accomplish.

---

[4]https://en.wikipedia.org/wiki/Behavior-driven_development#Behavioral_specifications

```
1    Feature:  admin creates a user
2        As an admin
3        I want to create a user
4        So that I ...
```

In this case, we try to imagine why the admin wants to create a user. Is it because she was assigned the task? Yes. Perhaps. But why was she assigned the task? So that a new person could use the system. But why do we want the new person to use the system? So they can share some portion of the work and hopefully speed up throughput. Now it is about saving time and money.

> So that we can speed our team by adding a new member

Most features come down to making money, making more money, saving time, saving money or avoiding loss. Consumer software may involve other motivations such as seeking love, entertainment or personal fulfillment, etc.

After the who what and why is clear, proceed to adding any more essential details. Quick, unformatted implementation notes or requirements may be given in a bulleted list such as:

```
1        - make sure text field has focus
2        - submit updates activity log
3        - prevent double submit
4        - user is redirected to account status page \
5   after completing
```

To Cuke or Not to Cuke?

Full Gherkin/Cucumber scenarios provide a powerful way of stating requirements. Cucumber stories consist of one or more scenarios, containing a sequence of Given/When/Then steps.

- "Given" steps set up the initial conditions.
- "When" steps describe something the user does.
- "Then" steps describe the desired or expected result.

Developers use various tools to actually execute these steps by driving a browser, simulated browser or by somehow simulating user interaction with the application directly.

Cucumber style stories and scenarios offer a great deal of precision. This precision can provide a lot of value whether or not developers treat them as executable code.

Cucumber is an investment. Maintaining and running a test suite with lots of Cucumber consumes a lot of time. The benefit of Cucumber seems clear when key scenarios are well-tested in continuous integration (CI) systems and when client or product owners learn to express themselves in Cucumber. Cucumber also proves handy for review purposes when onboarding a new team member or when returning to maintain or enhance a system after some time away. It can obviate the need for other more traditional specifications and design artifacts.

Experience shows us that 80% of the value from Cucumber testing may come from 20% of the tests. This means we want to use Cucumber or a similar testing tool to test the most common user paths and critical functions as well as sections of the system likely to break in integration. When quality is absolutely the top priority, we recommend more extensive cuking. Cuking everything however, could double or even treble the up-front cost.

Cucumber is not an excuse to skip other kinds of testing or more focused specs. You still need to drive the system through some functions in production either manually from time to time or using a browser automation tool. You also need to test logic using conventional unit tests or specs.

Producing Quality User Experiences

Developers of end-user applications must pay attention to the overall user experience if they wish to produce work of high quality. This topic could fill an entire chapter or standalone book. Here we will enumerate some of the principles developers should apply to improve the user experiences of their applications.

Decrease Cognitive Load

Good design reduces the need for training. Cultivate the ability to look at your application with the mind of someone who has no experience with it. Try to imagine that they were interrupted from their task and have just returned to the screen.

- Can they see where they left off easily?
- Can they see what to do next?

Use the user's language so they do not need to translate unfamiliar terms in their head. Eliminate jargon or any terms unique to your application. Improve the legibility of text so users may scan it easily. Make menus and navigation queues scannable. On every page, eliminate doubt about "where" the user is and what he or she may do there. Make it obvious.

Scan Don't Read

Users scan screens. Do not ask your users to read. Users scan at a glance. Reading requires effort.

Keep menus to seven items or less. Most people can scan and pick from a list of seven items at glance. Choosing from 8 or more choices requires stopping to read each one by one. This increases cognitive load. Prefer fewer choices.

Construct menu items or choices to communicate exactly what the User seeks. Use single words wherever possible.

Eschew word-phrases. Choose words that communicate specificity – as specific as possible while maintaining accuracy.

Remove Redundancy

Redundancy creates noise. Noise increases cognitive load. Our brains must filter out repeated patterns on a page in order to see the differences – "the essential information." This takes time and attention. Learn to spot this anti-pattern immediately and clean it up. It should cause you pain to see a UI with redundant information.

Design your field names to convey only essential information. If prefixes prove desirable in the database, hide them in the UI or group them in sections of related items so that a section label can hold the otherwise redundant text.

Respect the User's Time

Reduce the number of steps required to accomplish any task. Cut the clicks. Remove pages. Eliminate the need to scroll or leave the page. Make sure to present everything the user needs to know in order to perform an action at the time and place they need it.

Do not require the same piece of information to be entered more than once.

Do not pop-up dialog boxes requiring "remembered" information that is now hidden.

Do not ask the user to "remember" anything.

Do not use information from one dialog box to populate another subsequent dialog box in "wizard" like fashion.

Pay Attention to Detail

Pay attention to the tiny details. When clicking around the application to get somewhere that you want to test, take note of little things that are not quite perfect. Stop and fix them quickly if you can.

 Sometimes you need to keep your blinders on but if you never take them off, you will never notice what needs polishing.

Prevent the user from making mistakes whenever possible. Prefer this to using validation which requires the user to "go back" to correct something.

Keep Things In Place

Do not change the layout of the page during or after load. If user interface elements must appear or be hidden, leave empty space for them or place them in areas of elastic size which do not "push" other areas around. Avoid any distracting or uncanny motion that draws the eye.

Users memorize where things are so they can navigate an application faster. If something is not in the expected place, the user becomes annoyed or disoriented and must rescan the page to understand what to do. Once something is in a good place, leave it alone. Do not move other items around as you add features unless absolutely necessary.

Use the Visual Hierarchy of Importance

Users tend to follow the reading patterns of their primary language when scanning a page. For English readers, text begins at the top left of a page and proceeds to the right and down in a Z like fashion. In a scanning situation, pattern is generally that of an "F" shape.

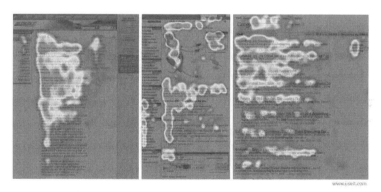

Heatmaps from user eyetracking studies of three websites. Courtesy of www.useit.com.

Place the most important information in the top-left corner area. Place the least important information on the bottom or at the bottom-right. For an in-depth discussion of this see 3 Design Layouts: Gutenberg Diagram, Z-Pattern, And

F-Pattern[5].

Empathise With The User

Feel the User's pain. Internalize the frustration they feel
when they have to click through six pages to get where
they want to go or enter some information for the third
time because the form "forgot" it and they feel like they
"lost their work." Understand what they are doing and why.

Imagine the environment in which they use the application.
Is it a noisy place? Is it crowded? Do they have interruptions? Is it going to be used for 5 seconds when boarding
an elevator? Or for 3 minutes while sitting on a couch? Or
for 30 minutes while sitting at a desk?

Manual Testing

Test the application regularly yourself. Step back and walk
through other parts of the application aside from those you
have recently worked on. Look at everything with fresh
eyes.

Enter realistic data. Enter invalid data. Do crazy unex-
pected things. Do not simply click the same path and enter
the same bogus test data every single time you go through
a scenario.

If you get frustrated with the speed of manual testing, write
a script to automate your browser against the live site.

---

[5]http://www.vanseodesign.com/web-design/3-design-layouts/

Use Realistic Seed/Test Data

When populating your development environment with data, use only realistic data. Do not enter "Foo" or "Blah" everywhere. Junk test data is a bad habit developers pick up when they rush without concern for quality.

You want to see what things will look like when the system is really used by real people for the intended purpose. This helps you to start testing and improving usability right away during the earliest stages of a project even when you are "just trying to make it work." If you need to, use some of the "factory" tools in your db/seeds.rb file to populate your database with realistic names and other data. Use numbers in the range of expected values. Do not put lots of $1.00 or $99,999,999.99 prices when you know most items will sell between $10.00 and $500.00.

Quality Under the Covers

I leave this section for last. Developers tend to want to discuss Quality in terms of architecture and adherence to best practices. This misses the point. At any given time you will observe other developers in the community recommend a host of "best practices." Do not take discussion boards comments as gospel truth. Evaluate each practice on its merits. Try it out and see how applicable it may be. Do not assume that a practice which seemed like a good idea on another project absolutely must be applied to a new project. Focus on the value to the Owner and the User.

Refactoring is important but gold plating under the covers is primarily for hobby projects. Professional development requires a certain amount of pragmatism.

On some level, we can understand code as a peculiar type of literature programmers write for each other. Code happens to have the constraint that it is executable by a machine. Look at your code. Is it legible? Are you going to understand it when you come back to it in six months or a year or two? Is someone else going to understand it? Even if they have no access to you? If the answer is clearly yes, then you have probably done a professional enough job on cleaning it up. Move on.

If the answer is "no," you have work to do. Refactor away.

Stay DRY. "Don't Repeat Yourself" is a useful programming heuristic. Do not obsess on it. If staying DRY is slowing you down too much, make an exception. Be pragmatic. Do not get sloppy.

Maximize Productivity

What Makes a Developer Productive?

We define our production as delivered value in the form of working software that does something useful or valuable for users and/or owners. Maximizing our productivity therefore involves maximizing the value delivered over time, or the pace of value delivery. Developing software consists primarily of exerting mental effort. Innate capability is part of the equation but there are many other factors which affect productivity. Some of these factors are entirely within our control such as personal habits and techniques. Others are within our influence, such as team dynamics, tooling, social and work environment, schedule, and requirements. (Yes we can influence work schedules and requirements!)

As professionals, we are responsible for our productivity – especially those aspects under our control or influence. We seek to control what is within our control, influence what we can for the best, and let the rest be as it may. This creates the peace of mind that helps produce good work.

Setting the Bar

When I was making the transition early in my career from Systems Administration into Software Development, I joined a startup with three other developers. Until that time, I generally thought of myself as the most skilled person in my little domain and I had quite an ego. I could set up and wrangle expensive servers, troubleshoot networks, build and deploy complex open-source packages, write object-oriented Perl client and server programs, make Java applets, create databases, even make dynamic websites. I thought I had it all down by my mid 20s. Working closely at that startup with three engineers who each had about 10-15 years more experience showed me just how far I had to go to attain anything like "mastery." One of these three was a man named Rand.

Rand previously worked at Hewlett Packard (before Carly) and before that at Apollo. He was a UNIX kernel guy. Hardcore. Everyone on our team looked up to him. We would do whiteboard design sessions and every time we walked out of the room the three of us would sort of shake our heads in amazement at how fast he could think through things. It was breathtaking just to keep up with him. He knew UML and several other diagramming techniques and could express his ideas quickly and elegantly. He knew all the design patterns. And he could code like a monster. He even typed faster than all of us. He had never used Java before but quickly became more expert than any of us. My Java experience was modest at best, and I think I was primarily hired due to my Perl knowledge (necessary for some legacy code we were building on), my operations skills and my willingness to forego my first 2 months' salary in exchange for equity since the CEO promised during my interview they "would raise money any day now."

Once I hacked the legacy code a bit, they assigned me to the front end of the project because I knew the most about HTML and stuff and of course, it was probably deemed the area where my inexperience would cause the least damage. One day I was struggling with the problem of how to generate dynamic web pages using these things called Java Servlets since we were writing our whole system in Java. All the examples consisted of concatenating strings containing HTML in Java which just seemed perfectly dreadful. This was 1997 and there were no Java Server Pages, Struts, EJBs or anything like that really. All Java had for web stuff was Servlets. (In my recollection it seemed about like Ruby's Rack interface only less useful – maybe more like plain CGI.) I had this vague idea of making something analogous to ColdFusion (which at that time was not written in Java and could not work with Java) or the "embedded perl" with which I was more familiar.

Rand observed my struggle on his way out one day. The next day, when he arrived precisely at 7am, (and he always arrived exactly at 7am and always left by 4pm) he dropped a 3.5" floppy disk labeled "Steve" on my keyboard. He said, "I wrote this last night. I haven't compiled it yet but it might help you."

Curious and a little frightened, I loaded the floppy which contained a single ~500 line Java file. I compiled it. Sure enough there was one type-o, perhaps left intentionally just to make me think he really typed 500 lines *after work* almost perfectly. As I began to read the code I saw that he had indeed prototyped a parser that would read in some HTML and look for special tags and which would cause some java code to be executed which could then operate on whatever was inside the tags and get replaced in the output. There were no logic errors. It was all nicely architected with a few well-conceived classes albeit in one file. I ran it on a simple example and it worked! With my skills at the time, it would have taken weeks or months for me to create a working version of that scheme.

I then used this as the basis for our product's web interface and proceeded to refactor, enhance it, and even release it as an open source project. It can be found on the internet archive wayback machine here.[6] Sadly, I did not give Rand the credit he deserved on that page.

Working with Rand and the others at Pubweb taught me a lot and gave me some key insights into what it takes to become a highly-productive developer. Rand set an entirely new bar of performance expectation. I wanted to be that good.

From time to time, I would imagine with my creativity how

---

[6]https://web.archive.org/web/19990125104405/http://www.wasp.org/

much more I could accomplish if I were also as disciplined, focused, and just plain fast as Rand was. I often wondered if he was just really smart or how much experience or habit contributed to his productivity.

If you have been fortunate enough to work with a really highly productive developer with many years of experience, use that to set a high bar of aspiration for yourself. Observe their habits and traits. Model them. Expect and demand high performance from yourself but realize it may take a decade or more to achieve your professional peak.

The "10x Developer"

We have all heard the myth of the "10x developer" or even the "100x developer". It usually goes something like this: "Some developers are 10 times as productive as the average developer." Let us assume that this statement applies within a given age or experience cohort. The profession tends to be dominated by people in their twenties with less than 5 years of experience and this can skew any discussion of "average" ability.

Most people who have been around software development long enough will concede that such a phenomenon is real and very likely true even when we consider only related age and experience levels. If you extend the comparison to "100x", what you might as well be saying is, "some developers do things that a typical developer simply cannot and perhaps will never be able to do." That is also very likely true although such people are indeed rare.

"100x" developers may be an example of the human phenomenon of genius – something which lacks precise definition. Although high intelligence may be a pre-requisite for acts or works of genius, statistically speaking, we all likely know one or several highly-intelligent people, perhaps even other software developers, who produce no recognizable works of genius. Clearly there are other factors at work.

Was Rand a "genius?" Here I mean "genius" in the casual sense of something by all probability we cannot hope to be. Ego aside, I'm pretty sure he wouldn't claim to be one. Certainly he was intelligent and quick-minded. But looking back now, from a similar point in my own career, his quickness of mind and mastery of the craft of software development is less of a mystery. Clearly he understood many of these other factors which lead to high productivity.

General Intelligence

Given that we have defined our productivity as a function of cognitive work achieved over time toward a specific end, we would be remiss if we did not address the question of general intelligence as it relates to the tasks we perform as developers.

Mainstream research has established that general intelligence is a real thing that can be reliably measured and that it is fairly stable throughout adulthood[7]. You have what you

---

[7]http://www.udel.edu/educ/gottfredson/reprints/1997mainstream.pdf

have and you can't do much about it. Sure, some efforts on the margins probably can make you score better or perform better at specific cognitive tasks or tests but that really doesn't make much difference overall. This can be a hard truth for some, but it is also kind of liberating when you think about it.

If you are modestly above average, then you have enough general cognitive ability to succeed in any profession, including software development, provided you are willing to work hard enough or train hard enough.

Programming, however, does require at least one specific mental capability which tests have identified and which can be readily ascertained in an interview. If you have written large working programs on your own, from scratch, you almost certainly have this capability. The following discussion will be of interest to all aspiring developers who have established their programming ability.

The takeway here is don't worry too much about whether you are smart enough. Do not spend too much time comparing yourself to others. The key is *do you enjoy programming*? If you can do it and you enjoy it, you have what it takes to succeed.

Efficiency of Effort

Once we accept the research regarding intelligence and its relatively fixed nature, to achieve greater productivity, we must focus our attention on making sure that our cognitive effort is effective. Let us define the effectiveness of our cognitive effort as our *Efficiency*:

Suppose one person, let's call her Jane, is twice as fast at a type of cognitive task as another person, Bill. Assume there is a long list of similar cognitive tasks for Jane and Bill to complete and these are the only tasks they are expected to perform. If Jane only spends 50% of her time over a given time period actually performing the tasks at hand and wastes the other 50% of her time, she will achieve only the same level of productivity as Bill. We will say that Jane has an efficiency of 0.5.

There are two great causes of inefficiency in software development:

1. Wasted Effort
2. Wasted Time

Let us define *wasted effort* as cognitive work in the form of software development that ultimately was unnecessary or which did not provide value. Examples might include such things as naively attempting to implement a poorly-defined feature and having to rework your approach several times due to misunderstanding. Other examples might include troubleshooting a bug in a 3rd party library that you ultimately decide not to use or developing an extensible framework as a hidden sub-project that will never be extended in the way imagined by the developer.

Father time shows no mercy and he stops for no one. Let us define *wasted time* as time that could be spent performing useful cognitive effort but which was not spent in any effort at all toward the task at hand. Examples might include that foggy period when you are "having trouble getting in the zone" or when you were interrupted by social call or an unnecessary meeting or office distraction. The most common example might be when you extended a short break beyond all reason because you decided to check Facebook, reddit or Hacker News resulting in a half-hour or more of distraction.

Understood this way, there are many ways we can improve our efficiency to maximally leverage our innate capabilities. You may even notice that some highly intelligent developers have extremely poor habits resulting in low efficiency. Their poor habits can rub off on their less-able peers such that the whole team would better off without them. A wise manager may recognize this and need not be especially intelligent in order see that by removing the "smartest" developer, they might raise the productivity of a whole team!

How much better could inefficient but talented people be if they were to learn to work in a more efficient manner?

Professional vs. Entrepreneurial vs. Heroic Development

Our aim here is to achieve consistently high levels of productivity as developers. All-nighters and manic deadline sprints followed by prolonged recovery periods are not part of our professional repertoire. You may enjoy such things from time to time but as you mature, personally and professionally, you will find them increasingly rare and unappealing.

Here we are not trying to hit isolated moments of peak velocity. We will not describe how to survive epic "death marches" or how to create revolutionary products on impossible budgets to meet ridiculous schedules.

If you are truly writing the Netscape browser for the first time or some other such revolutionary product, you may be called upon to perform extraordinary feats. This is entrepreneurial development at its most intense – it doesn't really describe professional development as we practice it.

 Heroic Development may be damaging to your health and personal relationships.

The fact is 99% of software does not intrinsically require extraordinary effort. Even most entrepreneurial development simply requires sound practices, well executed by sufficiently skilled people. The unfortunate frequency of calls for heroic effort results from poor planning, mismanagement, undercapitalization, and otherwise unrealistic expectations of those uninitiated to the realities of software development.

Habits of Highly Productive Developers

The following habits will help you avoid wasting time and will increase your cognitive efficiency.

Be Regular

Follow a consistent schedule. Be in the expected place at the expected time in the usual state of mind ready for work. Put in a consistent 8 hours of work in a day. Leave on time.

This sounds basic and easy and it is. For some reason a lot of developers, particularly younger ones, find this incredibly difficult. In general, regularity is a pretty good indicator of how well someone has his or her life "together" or in order. Older developers with spouses and families typically lead a more scheduled life and have less trouble with this.

Early in my career, I had other priorities, some of which conflicted with work much to the consternation of my managers. I placed a high value on flexibility and freedom. I enjoyed nightlife and would devour books until the wee hours. I allowed myself to sleep in accordingly. This was easier to reconcile with system administration and support work where I was on-call and would be regularly interrupted at night or odd hours to troubleshoot problems. Despite the flexibility this work afforded me, there was always some friction about my schedule.

As I desired to move into development, this was more and more difficult to sustain. Gradually I adjusted to accommodate what I perceived to be the needs of my employers. In the end I benefitted greatly from the change.

People who are committed night owls might prefer DevOps roles, entrepreneurial development, or support shift work over the normal-workday-schedule of a professional developer.

Professional development as we practice it is a team sport. At the very least you have your pair partner to consider. You may also need to coordinate with clients and others.

Being in the expected place at the expected time tells other people they can rely on you. When your teammates want to start work, they shouldn't have to wonder when you will arrive if they need to discuss something before proceeding. Your irregularity may also cause other team members to become irregular as well. Time spent waiting for another person to get back or show up, lowers your team efficiency. Arriving late when your partner leaves on time reduces your collaboration window.

If you are working with people across time zones, or in remote locations, regularity is especially important for building trust, ease of scheduling, and providing the greatest window for remote collaboration.

Leaving on time is important because if you don't have this book-end on your day, you will allow distractions to creep in. You will think you can just make up for some wasted time by staying a little late. A little late becomes an hour or two and then it becomes a regular thing. Very soon leaving late will lead to coming in late as well since you don't want to work too much and burn out. The cycle compounds.

Knowing that you only have 8 hours to achieve 8 hours' worth of work helps to push away distractions and focus on what's important.

Get Enough Sleep

Showing up to work without adequate sleep is almost as bad as showing up drunk. I say almost, because while some people can get by with one or two nights of poor sleep, cognitive ability degrades quickly with each hour of lost sleep. Prolonged periods of sleep deficit seriously impair cognitive function.

Extra strong coffee, a quick nap or other techniques can help compensate for the occasional off-day when sleep loss was unavoidable but these things should not be over-used. They are an anti-pattern – an indicator that something is off or that a problem needs to be addressed.

No useful development work gets done by someone who is drowsy. If you are pair programming, it is not fair to your partner who may feel compelled to shoulder the burden of your drowsiness or who may be distracted with the awareness of your non-contribution.

If you really are having a problem, excuse yourself and go home. Rest up and make sure you return bright-eyed and bushy-tailed the next day.

 Getting your sleep is part of your job. Anything that interferes with sleep, interferes with your job.

If you are having trouble sleeping at night and you have addressed the usual factors, such as

- noise or light in the environment
- other people disturbing your sleep
- disagreeable food or eating too late
- lack of exercise or over-exercise
- abuse of alcohol or drugs

and you are still having trouble sleeping to the point of causing drowsiness or diminished capacity at work, see a doctor to make sure you do not have a more serious condition.

Eat Right

We place diet in a similar category to sleep. Afternoon drowsiness is frequently related to the type or amount of food consumed at lunch. Overeating, sugary drinks, and certain kinds of starches or oils seem to cause drowsiness.

The goal is to obtain a fairly even energy level and state of awareness throughout the day. Dietary control is the primary means to achieve this. Macronutrient composition should include a balanced mix of protein, fiber, and fat. Many AELOGICIANS eschew rice despite the fact that it is a staple in the Philippines.

Excessive portions also contribute to drowsiness. A huge meal causes the body to divert more blood and oxygen from the brain to the stomach to facilitate digestion. This leaves less fuel for the brain to burn. "Food coma" results. In the extreme case you can actually fall asleep at your desk.

It seems the best state for brain operation is between just-barely-satisfied to ever-so-slightly-hungry. Alertness and cognitive function tend to rise about two hours after a decent meal until peaking just before the subsequent meal.

Defend Your Best Hours

I am keenly aware of my alertness levels throughout the day to the point that I try to make sure I am firmly "in the zone" and working on the hardest problem during the period of highest alertness. If someone must waste my time with something inessential or I must accomplish something less demanding of my cognitive powers, I try to schedule it during periods of lower alertness such as first thing in the morning, right after lunch or at the end of the day after I have finished up.

Once I consulted onsite with a client who needed significant work done to a large system which was poorly constructed by neophyte developers. The work required incredible focus because I was trying to be a Boy Scout and clean up and refactor as I went along – to leave the campsite better than I found it. The CTO was more of an operations guy than a developer and he had the unfortunate habit of calling meetings of his technical staff on a whim. On a day when I had a particularly difficult task ahead of me and a deadline bearing down, he interrupted me at precisely 11:00 AM – the peak of my awareness and productivity – to brainstorm something with a few people at the whiteboard. At the risk of upsetting him, I barely concealed my displeasure and asked firmly if this was urgent and whether I might be excused to complete the task I was working on.

Be firm even with your peers, your superiors and even your clients if necessary when it comes to defending your peak hours from interruption.

Cultivate Flow

> "Flow is the mental state of operation in which a person performing an activity is fully immersed in a feeling of energized focus, full involvement, and enjoyment in the process of the activity." - Wikipedia[8]

Almost all software developers know of the Flow state from experience. In fact, one might describe software developers

---

[8]https://en.wikipedia.org/wiki/Flow_(psychology)

as Flow-addicts. We enjoy our Flow but few developers learn the preconditions for attaining Flow and fewer still methodically apply that knowledge to enter Flow reliably. Developers tend to be haphazard about it.

Interestingly enough, the pre-requisites for Flow also seem to be things which are key to attaining high productivity genearally.

Here is what we require to enter Flow:

1. Knowing what to do
2. Knowing how to do it
3. Knowing how well you are doing
4. Knowing where to go (if navigation is involved)
5. High perceived challenges
6. High perceived skills
7. Freedom from distractions

Use this as a checklist when you start your day or return after a long break. You may be about to enter Flow when you feel like "the road ahead is clear."

When you sit down, state simply what you intend to do. If you don't know what to do, discuss with your pair partner, or pick something off the backlog.

Once you know what to do, make sure you have an approach in mind. If you don't know the general shape of the solution, try breaking the problem in to parts and figuring out if you think you know how to do each part.

Research any needed tools or techniques before setting out. Make sure you have a feedback system in the form of an automated test or a simple way to verify your successful progress, such as reloading a page. Lastly, make sure you know what to work on next or check that all the steps are at least vaguely lined up in your mind or listed in the work description.

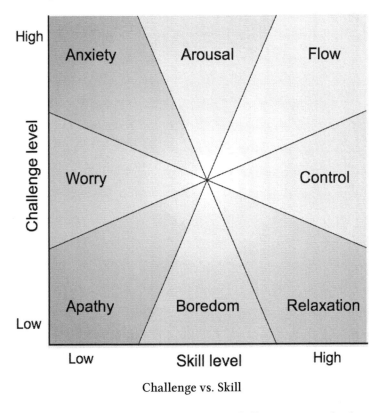

Challenge vs. Skill

If the challenge is too high or your skill is not matched to the task, bring this to the attention of your lead or manager

quickly. This makes it difficult to enter Flow or make efficient progress. Choose something else that is easier instead. Complete that before trying again or else leave it for a team member with a higher skill level. Or alternatively, ask someone with a higher skill level to work on it with you so that you can gain the benefit of experience.

If the skill required is too low, pair with someone for whom it will be a challenge and let them drive the effort or delegate the task entirely if your team structure will allow it. It is better to tackle something matched to your skill level than it is to drag out or perform poorly on a task about which you are apathetic. This is why teams should contain a range of skill levels and allow individuals or pairs to select their work appropriately according to difficulty and preference.

When you finish what you are working on and you only have an hour or two left in the day, choose something easy that you can complete in the time remaining. Do not choose a task you know you cannot complete unless you feel you could leave it in a good state to pick up when you return.

When to Take Breaks

Breaks are very important to maintaining high throughput. Structuring breaks well can give you a strong boost. Here are several indicators you need to take a break:

- you are too engrossed and lose track of the big picture

- you are out of flow and need to reset
- you have been sitting still too long

When you are deep in Flow, time passes quickly. Work on a particular problem may shift from Flow into a state of Hyperfocus. While this particular state serves a purpose – for example to keep all the relevant information needed to solve a problem in the conscious awareness of the developer – the motivation required to maintain this state can be "sticky." One can get stuck and lose sight of the larger task. This may lead to wasted effort.

If you feel like a dog attacking a bone and it is hard to pull away or for your partner to pull you away from the task, you know you are using hyper-focus well. Taking a short break can help you avoid the pitfall of wasted effort though. In this state of high intrinsic-motivation, problems appeal to your problem-solving appetite or obsessive-compulsive nature which do not really represent any value to the Owner or to the User. It is time to stop and step away from the keyboard...

Due to the time distortion of both Flow and Hyper-focus, one can become quite sedentary and not rise from the chair for an hour or two or even more sometimes. This is unhealthy.

For both health and efficiency reasons, we seek to take regular breaks. If you are unable to take effective short breaks often enough in a natural fashion, you may try one of these two techniques.

Pomodoro

The Pomodoro technique[9] involves using a timer to take breaks according a specific pattern or rhythm. It works as follows:

1. Decide on the task to be done
2. Set the pomodoro timer to n minutes (traditionally 25)
3. Work on the task until the timer rings; record with an x
4. Take a short break (3-5 minutes)
5. Every four "pomodori" take a longer break (15-30 minutes)

Clearly this dovetails well with the requirements for Flow. Shorter breaks are really preferred and we'll see why below.

 I strongly recommend that you stand up and physically walk away from your workstation during breaks. Do not simply open your phone, switch windows or check email. If you are properly hydrating yourself, then the longer (15 min) break typically coincides with a bathroom break.

Four sets of four pomodori make up a whole day. A well-structured day might look like this:

---

[9]https://en.wikipedia.org/wiki/Pomodoro_Technique

1. first set of 4 pomodori
2. morning break 15 min
3. second set of 4 pomodori (hardest work accomplished here)
4. lunch break (30 min)
5. after lunch set
6. afternoon break 15 min
7. wrap up set
8. unwind, go home

Assuming 5 minute breaks, this would yield 06:40 of work in an 8:40 work day with a total of 96 minutes break time not counting the lunch break. This is a base time efficiency of 81%.

Needless to say, this a very generous amount of break time and this method only works to produce a higher overall efficiency if each pomodoro is effective. That means every time you return and start a pomodoro, you are able to get right into the zone doing something useful.

Our base time efficiency rises to 86% if we shorten our 5 minute breaks to 3 minutes. This yields a total break time of about 66 minutes without lunch which is a little more reasonable. 3 minutes is short enough to go to the restroom swiftly. Any shorter is really impractical.

The short pomodoro break must not be extended. When you get up to get water or use the restroom during this break, focus on returning to work quickly. Engaging in unnecessary activity will likely overextend the break and unsettle your mind. Keep your mind clear so that you need less time to re-contextualize and re-enter Flow in the next pomodoro.

If you practice pomodoro, do not blow it by taking breaks except when pomodoro alarms you. If you need to use the restroom, wait until the break time comes. One mis-timed restroom break destroys a pomodoro, potentially wasting another 25 minutes or more than 5% of your day.

I do not approve of software tools that automatically lock the workstation screen during pomodoro breaks. In my experience, almost no one uses them properly. They become an annoyance and a Flow-destroying nuisance. Use simple timers either onscreen or offscreen with an alarm.

The 8 Glasses of Water Method

Train yourself to drink 8 glasses of water per day. This is the correct amount for hydration. Most people are chronically under-hydrated. In any case, if you drink 8 - 10 glasses of water in a day, at least 6 of those will likely be at work. You will likely have to use the restroom for each couple glasses of water you drink. You will rise almost hourly like clockwork to get another glass of water or use the restroom. No need for fancy timers. Just keep drinking water.

If you are pairing, try to make sure your pair is following the same break scheme. If your pair does not drink water, then try pomodoro or gently use your own bodily queues and the natural rhythm of the work to suggest good times for you both to break.

How to Take an Effective Short Break

We've already covered some of the advantages of short breaks, particularly for those who are experiencing high intrinsic motivation or who have a natural set up routine.

I maintain that it is necessary to physically get up and leave the workstation area for a break or it is no real break at all. If all you do is shift your gaze from the workstation over to your smartphone or personal computer, or worse, merely shift windows to some social network or news site in the background, you have actually harmed your productivity by breaking. When you do this, you are negatively programming yourself for distraction in your workplace. Get up and step away from the keyboard.

In our office we have a social standup table where you can specifically go to check email or do personal business on a computer. It is near the pantry so you can be easily seen and interrupted if someone has been looking for you but was afraid to interrupt you while you were working.

When you stand up to take your break, say out loud to yourself or your pair partner if you are pairing, a one-sentence summary of what you just did over the last 25 minutes or during the period since your last break. If necessary jot down any key information you will need to return to the task and then walk away thinking of something else or nothing at all.

When you return after 3 - 5 minutes, restate what you did last and what is to be done next. Then sit down leaving any unrelated thoughts or concerns that came to you over the break behind. If you are really into the problem you will likely have had related thoughts or insights to share with your pair partner when you come back. Share them.

When Not to Take Breaks

Do not take a long break if the system is down and users are suffering or if there is a critical bug that needs to be addressed immediately.

Do not take long a break if you have suffered many interruptions already and have not accomplished anything since the last interruption.

Do not take a break if you are distracted and unable to focus or get started. Instead, take this as a sign that you have lost Flow and prepare to reset.

Resetting

In stroke sports such as golf, or baseball, the player goes through a setup routine before making the stroke. This setup routine prepares the nervous and muscular system to make the stroke but it also prepares the mind. Interfering with the setup will frequently cause the stroke to miss or otherwise be deficient.

Software is the same. If we consider the stroke to be the work period you are about to sit down and complete, then following a consistent setup may help you to achieve a more consistent game.

When a golfer is off his or her game, he or she will put extra attention into resetting or going through the setup routine carefully.

Resetting can work like this:

1. Choose an item off the backlog that looks easy.
2. Then choose one that looks harder but still doable and position it afterward.
3. If nothing looks suitable, start breaking down the features or chores down until you have one easy one and one doable one. (Easy means that you would be able to complete it in one or two pomodoros or less than an hour.)
4. Make sure both of these features are well-defined and that you have all the necessary information to complete the task.
5. Then take your break.
6. When you return, start on the easy one.

With one success notched on your day, you can proceed to a more challenging item with confidence and clarity of purpose.

Avoiding Wasted Effort

Wasted effort is the enemy of productivity. When you are learning on your own or practicing to learn, no effort is wasted. You can learn something even from aimless exploration or troubleshooting. For the experienced developer, doing great work at high speed is quite frustrating if the work was unnecessary or ended up being of no value to anyone. Even if it was valuable but there was something much more valuable you could have done instead, the effort was somewhat wasted. In a professional context this is a real problem because someone somewhere is (or should be) paying a meaningful amount of money for your time.

Everyone on the team bears responsibility for avoiding wasted effort. Some factors here are entirely under the developer's control while others are only under their influence. In the end, if you as a developer are in a situation where too much of your time is wasted due to factors beyond your control, it is probably time to seek another job.

Question Everything

- Why do we need this feature?
- Do we really need all of this?
- Is this really the most important thing?
- Is this necessary for launch? (or the next release)
- What if we did a simpler version? (20% of the effort yielding 80% of the value)

These are the questions you should be asking. Good product managers welcome them – especially the 80/20 suggestions. Almost no one will turn down a good suggestion to deliver 80% of the value for 20% of the effort. Even if the other 80% of the effort is a must-do, the 20% that delivers 80% of the value should be prioritized and completed first.

If the answers aren't clear and unambiguous, you might want to work with the product manager a little to get some clarity. This is your responsibility as a professional.

Getting Started on a Difficult Problem

We have all been there. You have a looming difficult problem. It is so big you do not know where to start. You are now in the anxiety quadrant of the Challenge vs Skill chart. Much time is wasted here. This is when you are easily distracted.

I used to joke that I practiced Fear-Driven-Development. I would not start developing until the fear of the consequences of not starting overwhelmed my fear of starting. Sometimes I required down-right terror to get going. As in, "OMG I need to pay my bills and I need that client to pay and if I don't produce, he wont pay and then I will be in deep #$%^!" For the employee, fear of losing a job may cause a similar level of stress.

Sometimes it would simply be enough to imagine the unpleasant conversation I would have to have with an angry customer to explain a lack of progress. Once this fear reached a certain threshold, I would be able to push all other concerns out of my mind, even overcome the anxiety of not knowing where to start on something complicated, and just get going.

> *The journey of a thousand miles begins with a single step.* - Lao Tsu

When you are climbing a mountain, you do not have to have a complete map of the entire trail. It helps of course but the map is not the territory and there will always be surprises. Sometimes all you need is a glimpse of the peak to get started. Maybe the thing to do is just to gather up your gear and just start walking in the direction of the mountain.

Bounded vs. Unbounded Tasks

Estimation of large software projects has proven notoriously difficult. Without digging into the broad topic of estimation here, we recognize that much difficulty in estimation comes from the subset of the tasks comprising any project which we refer to as "Unbounded Tasks."

A *Bounded Task* is something that you know how to do in a reasonable amount of time. Your estimate may be off but it is not going to be wildly inaccurate.

An *Unbounded Task* is a something that you do not know how to accomplish in any reasonable amount of time. A task may be unbounded because it is well above your skill level or because you do not have required information or you do not have or know of the required tool to accomplish the task efficiently. It may require experimentation. In some cases it may require delving into algorithmic research or reading computer science papers. Some types of troubleshooting can be unbounded in nature. Fixing some classes of bugs can be an unbounded task. Responsible developers refuse to estimate these.

Unbounded tasks should be grouped and assigned to the category of "project risks."

In professional development we deal with unbounded tasks in one of a few ways:

1. Let the client deal with it
2. Find an expert
3. Timebox

Letting the client deal with it works for a few things. First, if there is proprietary IP or algorithmic development of a strategic nature, it is best for liability and other reasons if the expertise giving rise to the IP is directly employed by the client as part of their core team.

If the problem or task lends itself to specialized expertise, we may seek to access the expertise of someone for whom the task will not appear unbounded.

Timeboxing

When we must handle the problem of an unbounded task, we try to limit our exposure to the effect it will have on our velocity. The strategy for this is timeboxing. Give it an hour of effort, then put the problem away while you return to working on bounded tasks. Regular attention might chip away at the problem and it can enlist your subconscious over time. Awareness of the problem will spread beyond the team and other solutions or approaches may be suggested from the broader network.

If you are not sure how long something will take, do not just start it with a plan to continue until you are finished. Declare a specific stop time and have in mind what you will do next or return to before you start.

Speed Up Your Troubleshooting

Google quickly

Skilled developers often deride copy-paste programmers with good reason. In general, once someone has reached the level where they can be employed professionally, they do not want to simply copy-paste-and-try code solutions from the the internet. However, some observers have noted that better developers are often surprisingly quick to use search to solve some types of problems.

I specifically use search almost immediately when I have a unique-but-cryptic error message such as those sometimes found at the top of a stack trace – especially if it comes from a gem or third party component. Place the name of the component in the search along with the language or framework you are using and then the specific error. Stack-overflow to the rescue!

Immediately return to reasoning and troubleshooting if you do not see meaningful result in the first page of the result set.

Read The Source, Luke!

One of the key factors in troubleshooting successfully his having an accurate mental model of what is happening. When you lack a model, or your model is wrong, you will not be able to devise tests that yield useful information. Reading the source is essential to creating an accurate mental model.

The fact that we can even open and read the source is one of the greatest benefits of working on an open source software stack. If your problem is somewhere in the framework code, open it up in your editor and go right to the spot. Aside from the immediate value of solving a problem, every time I open good framework code, I learn something generally useful.

Other Strategies

When google and reading the source do not lead you to the answer quickly, try these other strategies. If you are pairing, your pair might split off and search more extensively for a clue on another computer while you continue instrumenting or pursuing a different strategy.

Our goal in every case is to zero in on the source of the problem as quickly as possible.

- Instrument the code to find the precise location
- Make sure you aren't dealing with bad data
- Return to a known clean state
- Divide the problem space and split up to work in parallel
- If you can order the problem space, use binary search
- Use version control by looking at the diff with the last known good version
- Step through with the debugger or REPL

These are some of the power tools you can use. 99.99% of bugs will eventually succumb to these techniques.

Progress in bug fixing often can be measured in terms of reducing the problem space. "Well, we know it isn't *that*."

> *Once you eliminate the impossible, whatever remains, no matter how improbable, must be the truth.* - Arthur Conan Doyle

Stick With The Crowd

When working with open source software components and frameworks like Ruby on Rails, you want to stay firmly in the mainstream and only step outside with full awareness. When you select little-used or obscure components or you try to do something in a manner different than that settled on by any significant portion of the community, your google searches will not help you. You will be on your own.

The first step when evaluating whether or not to use a component is: will this do what we need it to do? The second question is: is it popular? If it works and is commonly used, then you can proceed with some confidence. If it works but is obscure, or new, tread carefully.

Read the code. Decide if you are able or willing to support this component yourself. You may have to.

Go With the Smallest Delta!!!

Whenever you encounter a problem there will often be multiple valid solutions or approaches. Some will take longer. Some will be cleaner. Some will scratch some itch or other. Knowing which of several options to take is the hallmark of the master.

Here is the heuristic to apply 90% of the time: which change has the smallest delta?

Race horses often wear blinders to keep them from seeing what is going on all around them and getting distracted or spooked. Their mission is to win the race and stay focused on what is right in front of them.

In some situations I like to imagine we are in going in with our blinders on. We have a mission to accomplish and the goal is to get in and get out with as little distraction and pain as possible.

Think of the smallest code change as the most minimal and deft adjustment to the code that accomplishes the goal. The analogy from martial arts comes to mind: Motion in stillness. If a one-line change can fix it, that is probably the right solution. I always ask myself, what is that one small change that will do the trick?

Fixing something by writing tens or hundreds of lines of code when you could have done it with 5 or less, is probably not fixing anything. You are just making a mess. You might please an ignorant boss but you have done a disservice to the owner of the system. Don't waste your time. Get in, get out.

If you really feel something needs refactoring, make the minimal fix first and get it in the pipeline, then go do your refactor on a branch as time permits.

The alternative mode here is to play the "boy scout" – by which I mean, "leave the campsite cleaner than you found it." Sometimes this is the right thing to do. Particularly when you are confident that your changes will not break sensative code or when you have good test coverage. Editing something for clarity is fine, especially when you are reading code. But be sure you do not change the meaning! Know the difference between cleaning up and refactoring. It's easy to start with a small cleanup edit and then find yourself in an unintentional refactor that may waste precious time.

Open Your Gems and Libraries

Eagerly read the open source code you have – especially when you are troubleshooting something. For Rails developers this is as simple as "bundle open." Do it early and often. Definitely do it if your code is blowing up somewhere in the library. You will be better able to reason about a problem if you have all the relevant information.

Productivity Takeaways

1. Set a high bar for yourself
2. Avoid wasting time or effort
3. Avoid causing others to waste time or effort
4. Be regular
5. Get enough sleep
6. Cultivate flow
7. Take disciplined breaks
8. Timebox Unbounded Taks
9. Use web search effectively
10. Usually the smallest code change is the best solution

Pursue Mastery

A young boy traveled across Japan to the school of a famous martial artist. When he arrived at the dojo he was given an audience by the Sensei.

"What do you wish from me?" the master asked.

"I wish to be your student and become the finest karateka in the land," the boy replied. *"How long must I study?"*

"Ten years at least," the master answered.

"Ten years is a long time," said the boy. *"What if I studied twice as hard as all your other students?"*

"Twenty years," replied the master.

"Twenty years! What if I practice day and night with all my effort?"

"Thirty years," was the master's reply.

"How is it that each time I say I will work harder, you tell me that it will take longer?" the boy asked.

"The answer is clear. When one eye is fixed upon your destination, there is only one eye left with which to find the Way."

We pursue mastery because we pursue happiness. Observe the simple pleasure children experience when they discover a new skill or when they can feel themselves getting better at something. My younger son just learned to walk. He walks quickly now and every time he walks, he grins. He can't help it.

Somewhere along the way, every software developer of professional capability and many who never attain a professional level – every one of us – tasted the first joy of competence and control. We learned to navigate the logical world inside the machine. We learned the rules and made it do what we wanted.

Steve Jobs early on was asked to describe the Personal Computer – a novel concept at the time and one that required basic programming knowledge in order to use for even the simplest task. He described it in an unforgettable phrase as a "Bicycle for the Mind."[10] We do what we do

---

[10]https://www.youtube.com/watch?v=xqxWlvJ35yk

because we love to ride that bicycle and have learned to ride it well.

The continuing joy of discovery, the pleasure of making something happen, of being correct, of figuring it out, of seeing people use our creations, of gaining the respect of our peers – this is what drives us forward.

Enthusiasm will wax and wane repeatedly over the years of your career. You may even take a break from programming or from software development entirely. That may be a good and healthy thing to do. Experience in other fields and domains will make you a better developer.

When I started my career, I enjoyed programming so much that I did not want it to be my main job function. I felt that performing such a special activity on command for others for a wage would lessen the joy I derived from it.

My attention span was limited more or less to two days. I generally avoided writing programs that I couldn't finish in a single waking session. (Of course I could stay awake programming for 36 hours back then.)

My attitude softened in steps and by my mid-20s, I was determined to move beyond hobby-level programming and scripting in into "serious" full-time development. My experience with Java however, mostly confirmed my fears.

By my late twenties, I grew frustrated with software development. I found the tools were not fun to use. The little victories lost their charm. The political nature of software architecture made work a drag. Pointy Haired Bosses did not seem to appreciate my contributions. I grew distracted. The intrinsic and extrinsic motivation slipped away.

When the startup I worked at finally folded in 2002, I took the opportunity to travel and later to work for a while in real estate sales and home remodelling. During this period, I built a website and rediscovered the joy of programming during weekends in the library with my laptop. Eventually I jumped into PHP to develop a marketing website and after some success, I discovered Ruby on Rails. Ruby rekindled for me the joy I knew when I first learned to program and I have not looked back or questioned my career since.

We developers are lucky people. We get to do something that we love, that is difficult or impossible for many others, which is in sufficient demand that we generally receive above average compensation even for the barest competence. Our market is global and we can easily plug into the global economy. We generally get to work in air-conditioned offices in relative safety around mostly decent people.

If you don't work with decent people, or your office is uncomfortable, look for another job. Life is too short to spend your time with people whose company you do not enjoy.

Work Where Developers Are Valued

You will find pursuing mastery easier or more difficult depending on the work environment you choose. Choose to work for an employer who values your progress, who provides you with varied projects and experiences, and who attracts other talented and ambitious people.

Professional developers working for firms whose primary business derives from employing developers or whose business depends heavily on the technology they produce may feel especially fortunate.

Being a professional developer in a software studio or agency is akin to being a Creative in an Ad Agency or an Architect in an Architectural firm. Your product, your service *is* the business. This appeals to many talented and ambitious developers. In a relatively flat organization, developers will always be among the top class of employee and the technical promotion ladder may go all the way to partner.

In a startup or company with a great focus on technical product development, you may also enjoy high status or even an equity stake. Look at the top leadership. Is there a C-level technology executive? Was one of the founders technical? Do you admire their accomplishments and respect their skill? If so, it may be a good place to Level Up!

If you work in a large organization in the IT department, you may enjoy a comfortable life but you will never have high status since you will always work in a "cost center." Your career progress may not be as swift, your general marketability may deteriorate quickly if you are not careful, and your options for promotion past a certain point are generally limited to IT management. Entering management may require further advanced education in general business administration and may require you to let your technical skills atrophy. You will likely never move out of IT.

Professional software development in a consulting firm or studio is a good place to be but it is very competitive. You cannot coast for long. Either you grow your skills and ability or you fall behind. Either you produce value or you lose your job. There is little room for slackers in a professional firm.

Technology changes quickly. In five years, you may find that 50% or more of your day-to-day working tools and knowledge have changed. To stay in professional development you must engage in constant study and renewal. You must seek engaging projects or undertake "stretch" projects on your own. As you acquire experience and seniority, you may need to advocate for new technical directions in order to keep things fresh.

It takes focus to maintain or rekindle the joy that we all discovered early in our experience with programming. Working around like-minded, passionate, and talented developers makes it easier. Learning to do this in a professional context while consistently delivering value makes it sustainable for the long term.

Career progress requires understanding your capabilities and being honest about where you really stand. This helps you chart a direction and undertake work and projects that will get you where you want to go.

Evaluate Yourself

We strongly suggest all professional developers give themselves a thorough self-appraisal. We classify attributes that concern your professional development into three categories:

1. technical skills
2. transferrable abilities
3. personal qualities

Technical Skills include specific knowledge and understanding of tools, patterns and techniques as well as the ability to apply that knowledge to solve problems or produce working systems. Examples include "constructing a SQL left join", "configuring nginx", "defining active record scopes", "using rspec mocks", "composing photoshop mockups", etc.

Transferrable Abilities include skills or capabilities useful in other fields or contexts aside from software development. Examples include English grammar, effective google searching, strategic thinking, visualization, telephone manner, copywriting, time management, public speaking, etc.

Personal Qualities are those that describe your personality, temperament, and character. For example, extroversion or introversion, curiosity, diligence, passion, helpfulness, propensity to share knowledge, situational awareness, social polish, dedication, politeness, trustworthiness, etc.

 On a piece of paper, write down both your personal qualities and transferrable abilities that contribute to your strength as a software developer.

 Next, write any personal qualities that could hinder your professional growth. Think about the things you can do to improve in these areas. If you are not sure how to go about improving in an area such as time management, ask someone. You may easily find books on just about any topic of self-improvement.

Build a Technical Competency Map

A complete inventory of technical skills is beyond the scope of this book, however, we will describe a method for creating a technical competency map. Competency maps will be different for different kinds of software development.

We create the map with a four level hierarchy.

1. Development Practice (the root of our tree)
2. Functional Areas
3. Skill Categories
4. Specific Skills

Start with the first level which states the type of software development that you do. At my company, we would describe this as:

Full-Stack Web and Mobile Development.

Underneath this heading we would enumerate functional areas such as:

1. Ruby on Rails
2. Client-Side Javascript
3. Mobile Applications
4. WWW and Browsers
5. UX Design

6. Deployment
7. Development Tooling
8. Agile Process

Under the area of Ruby on Rails, we might further enumerate some skill categories:

1. Ruby Language
2. Active Record
3. REST
4. Rails Framework (excl. AR)
5. Rubygems
6. Testing
7. Performance
8. Security

Under the area of the Rails Framework, we would list specific skills such as:

1. User Authorization
2. User Authentication
3. Multi-tenancy
4. Internationalization
5. Asset Pipeline
6. Rails Console
7. Generators
8. ActionMailer

9. Background Jobs
10. Scheduling

In this way, we can expand every functional area and skill category into a large map of hundreds of skills. Taking a full inventory of hundreds of skills is a time consuming task. However, summary assessments at the skill category level may help to identify areas of weakness for further review and attention.

Through project selection or self-study, endeavour to become familiar with all areas of the competency map. Introductory knowledge is better than none at all. It can provide a starting point for quick study when required. Try to learn what is most important and pursue mastery by diving deep in the most leveraged areas of the competency map.

Find Your Level

Outside of companies with large technical operations, those in charge of HR generally do not give much thought to the career advancement of their technology professionals. Hardcore engineering companies like the old HP, IBM, Motorola and others had sophisticated and well-trodden technical ladders that ran parallel to the management track. Larger tech-friendly Silicon Valley companies such as Google also have well-developed technical ladders. This offers a career path for senior engineers and technical people who may not wish to give up their daily practice of engineering or technology in order to advance through management ranks.

Many less-sophisticated employers of software developers attempt to distinguish between "Senior Developers" and "Junior Developers." Sometimes they offer the "Architect" title to the most experienced. In product firms or companies where technology plays a key strategic role, a C-level position may exist for a hands-on technologist.

Unfortunately, all these titles come with a great deal of ambiguity. A "Senior" or a "Junior" is relative to the organization that granted the title and this presents a problem. For example, a company may offer the title of "Senior Developer" to someone as a compromise instead of a higher salary. It does not necessarily mean they are more skilled or experienced than a junior developer at another company.

A company which easily hands out titles may not help you to advance in your career as a developer. If they lack an objective criteria by which to judge the capabilities of technical talent, they can only give a loose guidance on how to achieve a promotion. This also politicizes promotion and makes it disorderly. Making up titles in lieu of salary diminishes the value of having that company on your resume or CV. Avoid employers who do this.

At my company, ÆLOGICA, we wanted to provide a clear ladder for technical advancement. This benefits the employee who wants to move up in his or her career. It also helps remove the hocus-pocus and dishonesty from salary negotiations. We fix a salary at each grade – take it or leave it. Negotiating skill is not really a factor in the compensation any individual developer receives. This also helps to diminish gender issues or bias by focusing on objective capabilities. The technical grade forms an input to our profit-sharing formula which also takes into account time-in-service.

In the event we made a mistake and hire someone at a level slightly above their capabilities, they simply wait a long time for promotion. If someone hires in well above their capability, they will be dismissed as a disappointment during their probation period. In this system it simply does not profit to oversell yourself.

At each stage of the ladder, we seek to describe the expected capabilities of the developer. We seek to develop both technical talent as well as soft skills. Advancement at the highest levels requires greater development of soft skills. At each level it should be clear what the developer needs to make it to the next level.

Each stage is tied to the developer's increased ability to deliver value. Our ladder applies to "Full Stack Web and Mobile Development" on open source platforms such as Ruby on Rails. Certain practices in this community may be less common in other communities but the tiers should translate reasonably well to other types of development.

Through observation and experience we identified at least 9 grades of software developer. There is room for variation within these guidelines. These are:

1. Developer Trainee/Intern*
2. Developer Apprentice*
3. Developer Associate*
4. Developer I
5. Developer II
6. Developer III
7. Senior Developer I
8. Senior Developer II
9. Master Developer

*not allocated for billable work except in an apprentice role

1. Developer Trainee/Intern

We begin with the developer trainee/intern who is characterized by Unconscious Incompetence – they don't know what they don't know. This person may have experience with one or two programming languages. The trainee/intern may not be familiar with source control, commonly used editors, or standard tools and techniques. They likely have not ever put a working system into "Production." This person may still be in school.

2. Developer Apprentice

A fresh graduate of computer science or of a technical discipline with proven programming skills is qualified to work as an Developer Apprentice. This type of person is characterized by Conscious Incompetence. They start to know the parts the puzzle but do not use them all effectively yet. The apprentice still requires a lot of self-study time to follow up on topics or techniques they may be exposed to through pairing.

3. Developer Associate

A developer who has been working professionally for a year or two will have established Conscious Competence. They know what they know. They can build and deploy a relatively simple application independently. The associate has hopefully begun to acquire good habits. They should be able to pair well and may start to become a good "navigator." They may still require extra time to research topics where they are weak.

> Up to this point, someone may play the role of the "Apprentice" for a team of AELOGICIANS. From this point onward, they may be considered a full team member, particularly when working alongside a Senior Developer.

Developer

The Developer I may carry his or her own weight in a pair. They may work solo under supervision or review of a senior developer. He or she will have achieved some mastery of standard tools and techniques. They will be able to estimate the relative complexity of tasks with fair accuracy. They will have acquired good development habits and practices.

The Developer I will tend to be focused on the problem at hand. They will benefit from being paired up with someone senior who has a larger field of view.

The Developer I has at least basic dev ops skills and should begin to help troubleshoot production issues. Developer I should have all code reviewed when working solo or when pairing with someone of the same or lesser ability.

Developer II

After several years of experience, depending on ability, the Developer II will have begun to explore advanced topics. He or she may be concerned with making good architectural choices and will be able to distinguish between options.

They may begin contributing to open source projects. After having worked on several different projects, they will have greater background with which to acquire domain knowledge more quickly.

The Developer II should be able to make helpful User Interface or User Experience suggestions. He or she may discern problems with specifications or anticipate problems. The Developer II will have learned to play the navigator role well and can push and challenge a pair partner. Estimation improves.

Developer III

Depending on natural ability after another year or two of experience the Developer III should be ready to lead a team. Developers should be moving through this stage generally between 4 and 8 years after starting full-time employment.

In the team lead role, we may expect a Developer III to help to apportion work and stay on top of what the other team members are doing with an eye to improving the overall throughput of the team.

The Developer III should set an aggressive pace and should communicate a sense of urgency to teammates. The Developer III will have learned to make reasonable assumptions to fill in the blanks and will consciously make tradeoff decisions. The Developer III will break down work into manageable chunks and will sequence them for better throughput.

The Developer III should be proactive in communication and easily understood by clients and collaborators. The Developer III is very conscious of his or her own efficiency and seeks to remove blockages. The Developer III encourages good habits in others and should feel confident enough to draw attention to slackers.

Senior Developer I

After gaining between 5 and 10 years of working experience, a developer should be able to lead a team confidently and to design larger systems well. We place a great emphasis on soft skills at this point in order to keep the demands on management as light as possible.

A Senior Developer I should be able to lead a team confidently and smoothly, anticipating problems. An important trait I look for in a Senior Developer I is that he or she must inspire confidence in clients. We also want to see prudence and caution in DevOps as well as the utmost in trustworthiness.

Strong code review skills, command of best practices and good architectural instincts are required at this point. He or she will be responsible for reviewing and approving the output of other team members. Third party reviewers should have little to complain about the output of a Senior Developer I.

Senior Developer II (8-10+ years)

A Senior Developer II will begin to look beyond his or her immediate project and team. He or she should be able to track multiple projects and be attuned to their non-technical needs (e.g. staffing). A Senior Developer II should be able to jump in and take over roles in unfamiliar projects quickly with little or no ramp-up time.

A Senior Developer II can navigate organizations effectively to achieve necessary cooperation and understands the business aspects of development. He or she should make more significant contributions to open source or to the profession through speaking or publishing. A Senior Developer II should be able to design and optimize deployment architecture production systems for high performance.

A Senior Developer II knows the rules and when to break them.

Master Developer (10-20+ years)

I call myself a Master Developer – first of all because that is my role – I lead other developers and run a firm consisting primarily of developers. I choose to emphasize that rather than my executive position because I see myself as a first among equals. We are all developers.

I also believe the title implies something about my capabilities. I know quite a few in my peer group who deserve the title at least as much. They are generally the ones who last into their late 30s and 40s and are feeling stronger than ever in their abilities. They are hands-on CTOs, veteran leaders of large projects, builders of big systems, maintainers and leaders of prominent open source projects.

A Master Developer can take simple high-level requirements and build an entire system. He or she knows just what to ask to obtain the information necessary to build a proper solution. He or she will be able to recruit and lead teams of senior developers through reputation, personality and merit.

A Master Developer can diagnose problems with teams after a short period of observation. He or she quickly understands new systems, requirements, and domains. A Master Developer applies design thinking to deliver better user experiences and higher perceived quality. He or she will zero in quickly on the essential questions or problems and wastes little time. A Master Developer may also know better which projects not to pursue.

A Master Developer should inspire great confidence and is well suited to run or lead a technology organization.

Move Up

By spelling out a clear technical ladder with a profile of capabilities at each step, we make expectations clear. If your workplace does not have well-defined ladder like this, encourage them to create one or go to work for a company or workplace that does.

Without a ladder you have little guidance for what to do to earn a promotion or to advance your career. Your only option may be to look for a new job. Every employer of skilled developers cares about retention. Employers benefit from having a technical ladder through retention and easier recruitment. It will help attract good people who are sincere about their career progress.

Assuming you have found somewhere with a technical ladder and you found a place on that ladder, look at the next step up. Can you imagine that description fitting you? What do you need to do to get there?

Directed Study

Occasionally we must make a concerted effort to pick up a new technology or programming language. The Pragmatic Programmers (a publishing house) recommends learning one new programming language every year. Despite the fact that the proponents of this maxim make their money selling programming books, this is sound advice. For some this may be too much of a time committment. That is understandable. Becoming proficient in a programming lanugage is no small feat. However, if you have not sincerely tried a new langauge in two or three years, you are doing yourself a disservice and you may find yourself falling behind your peers. You will certainly lag the best people in your profession.

Some new systems or techniques can be grasped in a day or two depending on ability. Others require more practice. Learning a new language, framework or platform may require hundreds of hours. You may have to be pretty clever to convince your employer to let you spend hundreds of hours learning a new technology. If you a fast learner, the technology is cutting edge, and there is a strong business case for its use, you may get away with it. If you get this opportunity, take it.

Absent such employer-sponsored study, you may need to spend your own nights and weekends for a while. To keep ahead of the great mass of lazier developers you'll need to do this at least every couple years. If you neglect to do it, you will wake up one day while passing a major milestone, say age 30 or age 40, with that sinking feeling that your skills are going stale.

You may be highly compensated at your present job but what would another employer pay you to work on a system with which you are less familiar? If the answer is not much, the alarm bells should be ringing. Either shore up your job security or start a side project in a new technology platform.

Just in Time Learning

You will encounter many situations in which you need to rapidly learn something new. This is not necessarily the right time to deep-dive and go heads down for weeks. You need to be pragmatic.

Your mileage may vary but here is the pattern I use when I need to pick up something quickly.

First, determine how much you need to know. Be absolutely clear on the goal. You may want to use an unfamiliar tool to do a job or solve a problem. The tool is a means to an end. You are not trying "master" it. You are trying to learn enough about it to do what you need to do and move on.

Next, look for a survey source. If the technology is mature enough to have a book written about it, find the ebook version. Technical books are pretty formulaic. Usually you can read the first two or three chapters to get the big idea and use the rest as a reference. For less mature technology search for a blog post. If you're lucky, someone may have written a nice one. If not, consider writing an intro post of your own as part your survey of the topic.

Once you read any survey material, pick a simple exercise and try it outside of your current codebase. If it becomes clear how to apply the tool or technique to your original problem, go ahead and do it.

If you still do not see how to apply the technique, try to imagine a more complex usage than the examples provided in any material you have read. Try to implement that outside of your codebase. If you still do not see how to use it, consider alternatives. Perhaps the tool is not applicable to your problem.

Give Back

We benefit greatly from the programmers and computer scientists who have come before us. The complex software systems that power our computing systems and devices represent millions of hours and thousands of years of human effort. These vast logical assemblies comprise some of the most complex machines created by mankind. In the open source world, much of this effort had no direct or immediate commercial motive.

I found my professional home in the Ruby community and I remain an enthusiastic supporter primarily because I feel the community strikes the right kind of balance between public-spirited activity and pragmatic business-orientation. We all have to earn a living but we are also part of something larger than ourselves and the strictly financial interests of our businesses and employers.

At one of the earlier Rails conferences I attended, David Hannemier Hansen (DHH) described the "surplus" we produce from doing sufficiently valuable work or by using tools that make us much more productive than "average." The surplus takes not only the form of money but also time and other things. He encouraged those listening to spend our surplus wisely and creatively – to do new and interesting things with our lives.

Traditionally we see businesses as (monetary) profit-maximizing machines. Theoretically their job is to earn as much profit as possible for their shareholders. Truely great businesses however are not only profitable for their shareholders but also produce great "returns" to their community, employees, customers, and even society at large.

Likewise, individually, we ought to look beyond the personal gains or private benefits of the work we do to try to make a broader impact or return.

The easiest way to give back may be to share your knowledge through a blog or through mentorship. Volunteer at outreach events or teach a class. Ask your employer if you can do some work for a charitable organization or use your surplus time to do so. Not everyone is destined to create a framework which vastly improves the efficiency of millions of workers and consumers, but we can each find worthy ways to spread the surplus created by our talents and the contributions of others.

Be Professional

Professional software development is a service occupation. We offer *our services* to clients, customers and employers in both a professional context and manner.

Professionalism in software development entails both style and substance. It involves both how you represent your firm and how you conduct yourself. Every customer contact, communication or touch point presents an opportunity to create a good impression. As professionals we always seek to create a good impression. Surface impressions however take a back seat to rectitude and professional conduct. We exhibit rectitude and professional conduct in matters of trust and in situations when others are not necessarily looking.

Be of Good Character

Professional developers often find themselves in positions of trust. The more skilled and experienced you become, the more important your character becomes to your job function and qualification.

Many licensed professions have explicit ethical standards and boards to adjudicate matters of concern. Paradoxically, these professions are also often rife with unethical behavior.

In software development, we do not have licensure and we do not have professional bodies to adjudicate disputes or punish ethics violations. Right and wrong may not be black and white in many technical contexts where arguments for different technical solutions have merit. Right and wrong however are easier to discern in the handling of confidential information, intellectual property, systems security, contractual obligations, and the operation of systems essential to functioning businesses. Professionals need to have a clear grasp of ethical conduct in these areas.

At my company, we are keen observers of character because it is necessary to the smooth functioning of our business. It is also very important to our clients. One need not have a great imagination to see how low-character individuals are unsuitable for professional employment no matter their technical expertise.

> If you observe an ethically dubious behavior in your coworkers, report it directly to management. If you are in a small company, report it to the owner or CEO. If you find the owners or management perpetrating or tolerating such behavior, find another employer ASAP – nothing good can come of staying where you are.

Here are some simple rules to keep you on the straight and narrow path:

1. Don't steal.
2. Don't lie. Don't cover up your mistakes. Own them.
3. Protect your company, clients, customers, and users.
4. Be nice. Treat people decently and with respect.

That is pretty much it. #4 is the golden rule. You can derive the others from that.

For consideration of a more thorough ethical code suitable for professional developers, consult the Association for Computing Machinery Code of Ethics[11]

Fortunately, software generally, and open source in particular seems to attract people who exhibit generally ethical behavior. Maybe I am just lucky but in over 20 years, I have yet to run into any obvious, acute ethical failures by skilled software developers. I think we could use some improvment however, in concern for the broader impact of our work on society.

I joined the ACM, in large part because I want to support one of the few voices for ethical behavior in our profession.

Information technology is incredibly powerful. Society has not yet come to grips with some of the implications of rapid information technology adoption.

---

[11]http://www.acm.org/about/code-of-ethics

Some of the highest profile firms building the future we all seem destined to live in also employ armies of young engineers who lack the maturity or depth of life experience and perspective to understand the full implications of what they are building.

How many "big data" practitioners subscribe to this item from the ACM Code of Ethics:

> *1.7 Respect the privacy of others.*

How many offensive "information security professionals" employed in the government sector comply with this:

> *2.8 Access computing and communication re-sources only when authorized to do so.*

Such people can say that they are authorized by their superiors and perhaps under some law but the only people who may legitimately grant access to information systems are the owners of those systems or their agents.

We are responsible for the effect of our work on people and society. As professionals, we must understand the implications of our work and choose projects and employers accordingly.

Create a Professional Impression

Your ability to create a professional impression contributes to how your managers, clients, and coworkers perceive your value. Your professional aspect will help determine your long term success almost as much as your ability.

Many behaviors and choices affect your ability to create a professional impression. It can mean something different in different contexts. For example, if you are working from home and communicating through a chat room, your attire may not be important – attention will be focused on other aspects of your "presentation." On the other hand, if you have a daily standup video chat with your team or a client, you should probably wear a decent shirt or clothing, regardless of your work location.

Most of this is to varying degrees, common sense. However, developers who have spent their time mastering the intricate world of the computation, often benefit from a little coaching and polishing on the finer points of human interaction.

Be Punctual

Punctuality creates an impression of reliability and contributes to efficiency in a professional, collaborative environment. When your colleagues and clients learn they can rely on you, your perceived and actual value increases.

People who are terminally late may be perceived as unserious and unreliable. Collaborative tasks stretch out due to delays communicating with the unpredictable individual. This diminishes the value of their talent and contributions.

Communicate Effectively and Politely

Everyone appreciates clear communication. Take extra effort to make your communications precise and efficient. Do not use technical jargon where unnecessary or when the other party will not understand. Do not waste the time of others. Do not create unnecessary request-response cycles.

Try to anticipate all your needs so that you can ask for multiple things in one communication transaction. This way your correspondents can batch up their interaction with you. Every communication involves a "context switch" and it has a cost. If you repeatedly ask for information in little installments, it makes communicating with you very expensive.

> High-value professionals communicate tersely and competently. For example, we retain a very expensive attorney. His emails are always short, well ordered, logical affairs with a clear prompt for action. Endeavor to make your communication similarly brief. Brevity oozes competence and whispers value.

If you have an accent in English, try to remove or reduce it. Emulate those around you who have a neutral accent or more polished English. In the global marketplace for developers English skill multiplies your value. Even native English speakers from countries with pronounced accents such as India or even Scotland will benefit from toning down the accent if they wish to collaborate with people outside of their home country.

Conference Call Demeanor

Remote collaboration is a fact of life for the professional developer. We use conference calls, video conferences and screen sharing sessions to communicate with our clients and other developers. Be responsive and alert. Take the lead if necessary. Keep conversations on topic when appropriate.

Choose the Right Medium

Different communication methods have different properties which make them appropriate to varying situations. In general we prefer to use "high-bandwidth" communication for unstructured communication and collaboration. What do I mean by this?

Low bandwidth methods include:

- sms
- chat
- email
- email with attachment

High bandwidth:

- phone call
- audio conference call
- video chat
- skype w/ screenshare
- in person face to face
- conference room with whiteboard
- pairing

When two developers are working on a technical problem together, to resolve it as quickly as possible, they should sit together at a pair programming station. Emailing each other ideas to try out will be very slow.

Likewise, if you need to clarify a requirement with a product manager, a quick phone call will allow you to sort it out faster than in email or chat. If you need to leave an audit trail of the conversation, make an annotation in your project tracking system or send a follow up summary of the conversation.

Try to be aware of or even anticipate when communication is slowing down work due to using the wrong medium. Suggest switching to a better medium when it will help things move faster.

Be Responsive in Chat

Despite our preference for high bandwidth, chat sessions provide a lot of value and form an essential part of our repetoire. Creating a good impression in chat is not difficult. In most cases, it simply means responding quickly. When a client or other party asks you something in chat, try to acknowledge the message quickly. If you are busy, it is perfectly okay to tell them you will get to it in a few minutes when you come up for air. If the communication is urgent, a pair can be helpful by breaking off to chat while the other member pushes ahead with the task at hand.

Use a chat or IM account specifically for work. Do not give that account out to your friends. Ask people to refrain from messaging you if they are too chatty and distracting. Watch out for noisy group chats. Leave them if they become too noisy or do not add value.

Use Email Properly

Email is incredibly useful but it is also one of the most abused communication techniques. There are only a few basic reasons to compose and send email in a business context:

1. Informing others about something (unsolicited broadcast)
2. Responding to a request for information
3. Requesting information

Prefer brevity in all cases. If you find yourself writing more than two or three sentences, stop and chop. What do you really need to say? No one wants to read your wall of text. Stick to the facts. Strip it down to essentials. ELI5.

I often simply delete long emails, especially anything with emotional content. If you feel compelled to write a long email detailing your feelings about some complex issue or interpersonal relation, you probably need to discuss the issue in person or on the phone. Walk over and invite the person for a chat, go for a walk, or worst case call them. Writing about it may help you clarify your thoughts ahead of a conversation but just because you wrote such an essay doesn't mean you need to send it along.

Mind others' time. Limit your CC lists. Feel free to drop people from a CC list if you are replying and anticipate responses. Make sure you know everyone on the CC list. Do not reflexively Reply-All every time.

Avoid casual swearing, trashy or offensive language. Avoid making excuses. No one cares. Excuses do not justify anything and they distract from whatever other information you needed to convey.

Here is an example from a real email that should have been worded differently:

> "Sorry for the really late response. I was out of town and I just got home a while ago. I fixed it 12 hours ago, but I wasn't able to send an email because I had crappy internet. I've also attached another script that gets the status of a message based on the ID that the API returns."

This would better stated as:

> "Sorry, just saw this. Here is a script that gets the status of a message based on the ID that the API returns."

Remember the TMI rule – too much information. Less is more.

Standups

The Agile movement popularized the concept of a Standup meeting. They are short meetings which are conducted while standing. They should be short – 10 to 15 minutes or less. If people sit down, they are no longer standups They are meant to convey essential information, ensure everyone knows what to do, and to illuminate any conflicts or holdups.

Standups are not meant to report status or to make all the work you did yesterday sound REALLY IMPORTANT AND DIFFICULT. Do not let some self-important politician yammer on about what they already did. The key is to remain forward looking with a focus on the very short term. What are you doing in the next few hours and do you need anything from anyone else? If the team is unaccustomed to this format, anyone can exhibit leadership and put things on track by asking each of the others these two questions.

Ideally everyone should get a chance to speak, although they may not opt to say much. The idea is that in a small enough group, everyone no matter how timid or softspoken, should have a chance to speak up. Larger groups may pass a token around to ensure everyone gets a turn.

Manage Your Time

Effective time management marks the professional in any field. Software development is no different. We covered most of the techniques we practice for efficiency in the chapter on Maximizing Productivity.

Managing your time as a software developer can be quite different from how other professionals manage their time. Non-technical managers or collaborators often do not appreciate this.

A typical manager or executive goes by an hourly or half-hourly calendar or daily schedule. His or her planner fills with meetings or appointments beginning and ending at specific times. He or she may block off periods for handling email or other administrative tasks.

Software development consists of an open ended series of tasks that take as long as they take. Without extensive up front analysis, we usually wont know exactly how long something will take until it is nearly finished or at least well started. Starting and stopping is expensive. We lose efficiency whenever we have to put our work away before we are finished. Our velocity takes a hit when we must put our work out of mind for a period longer than a few minutes or if we are required to bring a similar level of attention on something else. Returning to an unfinished task and getting up to full speed or "where we left off" can require a half-hour or more.

I have never seen anyone effectively "multi-task" while developing software. If someone tells you they can do it, they are deluding themselves. If something else requires your continuous partial attention, put your software development aside and find another useful task more amenable to interruption or partial attention. You can perform UX review, manual testing, etc., with partial attention.

To manage their development time effectively, developers must push their communication and non-development tasks into either the start of the day or the end of the day. The goal is to create at least two or possibly as many as 4 unbroken stretches of at least 2 hours duration. These periods support a meaningful amount of work.

Software development requires such concentration that we will often avoid starting any serious task if we only have 15 minutes before the next interruption. This means that scheduled interruptions should be grouped together. If one appointment ends and you have a 30 minute slot before the next one, more than likely nothing useful will get done in those 30 minutes. From a development perspective, they will almost certainly be wasted. We want to avoid this. If you cannot avoid gaps like this, find other useful non-development tasks to fill the time.

Handle Personal Business During Scheduled Breaks

Personal business is no different from any poorly considered interruption by management. Discourage your family or friends from trying to call you or chat with you during the day. Condition them that you will contact them if you are free. If they do contact you, tell them simply when you will be coming up for air and call them back then. Pretty soon they will adjust to accommodate you and only reach out to you for emergencies.

Simiarly, set personal appointments during a lunch break or after or before work. Avoid situations which will cause you to leave your work in the middle of a productive period.

Feel Urgency

Most importantly, you must feel that your work is important and that your time is valuable. Let your actions communicate this to people around you.

If you make the mistake of thinking your time is not valuable, you will not pay attention to making little efficiency gains. You will not be annoyed as you properly should be at people or things that waste your time. You may even lapse into less professional behavior or begin to waste others' time. At the extreme of this is the "tomorrow" or "mañana" culture found in some communities. Fight this mentality wherever you find it in your workplace.

If you are not enthusiastic about a task, try to look forward to getting it done already so you can move on to something better. If you drag out a task or procrastinate, you waste your own time, not just your employer or client's time. All the time you waste diminshes your value and postpones or delays useful learning that could increase your value.

When you think about how much you earn and whether or not you could be earning more, ask yourself if you are really making the most of your time and feeling urgency when you work. Employers and clients will notice it if you feel urgency and show it. In any decent meritocratic environment, you will advance.

Pair Pragmatically

Pair programming is still one of the most controversial techniques to come out of the Agile movement. Non-technical managers often doubt its effectiveness. Reclusive programmers accustomed to a high degree of autonomy and very little scrutiny or oversight, may resist opening up and sharing their work and thought process so completely.

It is very different from the cliched developer working alone with a door shut or in a cubicle or bullpin with headphones on. Among those who practice it properly, there is little doubt about the utility and value of the technique.

What is Pair Programming?

Pair programming as we practice it at ÆLOGICA, consists of two people sitting at one powerful computer with a single large 27" or 30" monitor. Developers may opt to keep a personal laptop to the side of the main computer for use in looking up documentation or performing quick research.

Two keyboards and two mice are connected to the single computer. Either person may control the computer though only one person is typing or controlling the mouse at any given time. The two developers will continuously discuss the problem at hand and will take care to vocalize their thoughts to share with the other person. Control passes back and forth naturally in the course of the work or possibly according to an agreed cadence. Both "hogging the keyboard" and partner-disengagement is frowned upon.

Ramon and Cecille pair-programming. Ramon is navigating, Cecille is driving.

The person who is actively typing or who has their hand on the pointing device may be referred to as the "driver." The person who is not typing may be referred to as the "navigator." The phrase "let me drive for a second" or "you drive" is commonly used to switch roles.

Why We Pair

The main benefits to pair programming include:

- fewer defects, better designs
- knowledge is spread around the team
- mutual accountability
- better adherence to conventions and best practices
- faster convergence to solutions for complex problems
- less time spent "stuck"
- higher engagement and enthusiasm
- less time wasted on non-development tasks

The cost of pair programming according to some studies, seems to be about a 15% in the form of an up-front decrease in the apparent velocity as compared with each developer working solo. However, the higher quality leads to reduced re-work, lower ongoing maintenance costs and perhaps delayed obselence. This increases the value of the software asset. Higher employee satisfaction leads to lower turnover. When turnover occurs, knowledge is more distributed throughout the organization. Pairing also makes it easier to bring new developers on and make them productive right away. This means any given person less essential to a particular project. Managers should appreciate all of these things.

I submit that significant commercial software development is rarely undertaken without the expectation of 10x or more return on investment. If a given project cannot accept a 15% pay-it-forward tax to "do things right" and produce a more maintainable, lower-defect system, with employees who are happy to continue to work on it, then one might wonder if the development should be undertaken at all. This holds true whether the tax is paid through pairing or through other techniques aimed at addressing the same problems.

We believe that by pairing pragmatically as opposed to dogmatically, we can realize most of the benefits of pairing without necessarily paying the 15% tax.

How Pairing Saves Time

Non-technical managers may have trouble visualizing how pair programming can be anything other than twice as expensive as "solo" programming. The naive person observes two people sitting at one computer and imagines that their production will be halved. An illustration and analogy from sport will help explain the fallacy of this thinking.

As we discussed earlier, there is a notional Minimum Essential Effort (MEE) in the development of any feature or the accomplishment of a software development task. Let us represent this on a 2 dimensional surface as the straight line from the starting point to the ending point.

Ideal path of Minimum Essential Effort

This is much like a leg of a sailboat race between two marks placed in the water. The MEE is the "perfect course" which would lead to the shortest distance traveled.

We measure our rate of progress in sailboat racing with the term "Velocity Made Good" (VMG) – that is speed toward the mark. One rarely can steer a course "straight for the mark" – the wind may shift, other boats may get in the way, current may push the boat one way or another, the fastest point of sail may not be very close to the ideal course, etc. There are many factors.

A sailboat racing crew may consist of at least several people: one or more to handle the sails, one to steer, and one to navigate. A few more may be handy for "rail meat" but here the analogy breaks down. Suffice to say that a boat with at least two or three crew focusing on their individual roles – ceteris parabis (all other things being equal) – may be more speedily sailed toward the mark than a single-handed vessel where one individual performs all the roles.

Software development is a multi-dimensional activity and forward motion does not always imply progress toward the desired end. Direction is very important. The following diagram shows how a pair may stay on course and drastically shorten the actual calendar and clock time expended on a task.

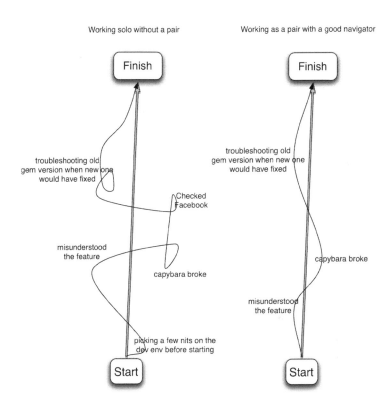

Working solo without a pair   Working as a pair with a good navigator

Solo vs. Pair Programming

With this visualization and the benefits we hope to obtain

by pairing firmly in mind, let us proceed to discuss guidelines for pairing pragmatically.

When to Pair

Here are the occasions when we almost certainly want to pair:

- When two heads are better than one

  Complex problems with a lot of context may benefit from pairing. If you you feel like you need to "talk it out" you probably should pair. If you are confused about a requirement or need to make a guess about something and the customer or product manager is not available, pair. If you are unsure about how to properly test or structure something, pair. If you are working with an unfamiliar system or subsystem, pair. If you are struggling with your tooling and you suspect other developers have resolved the problem or that your problem affects everyone, pair.
- When you intentionally want to transmit knowledge or technique
- When deploying to production

  Depending on the complexity of the system, how many users it has, and how much money can be lost with an outage, less experienced people generally should not deploy to production alone. Two heads are more likely to spot a problem quickly before irreversible steps are taken. Discussing the plan explicitly with someone who bears shared responsibility for failure may highlight problems or risks before they occur.

- When reviewing code or pull requests or making a large commit

   Someone will have to look at the code later one way or another. It is better to inspect it now.

- When on-boarding a new team member

   There is no faster way to get someone new up to speed.

- When you are having trouble staying focused

   Your pair can help you focus on the chore. People hesitate to interrupt a pair of people who are obviously engrossed in a task, whereas people frequently feel justified in interrupting someone who is working alone. Discussing the overall plan with someone can help clear the road ahead.

- When you are not sure what you should do

   Your pair probably knows what to do or at least can help you figure it out quickly. Two people can more easily "saturate" the design space or come up with varied approaches to a problem.

When Not to Pair

Pairing pragmatically means that while we prefer to pair, we recognize there are some occasions where pairing may not be beneficial. Here are some times we recommend breaking off:

- When you need to cover ground as quickly as possible

  Quality isn't always an overriding concern. Occasionally you just need some stuff working quickly for a demo. Or occasionally a critical item comes up but you do not want to disrupt progress at the main front of development. Split up.
- When you can divide and conquer the problem space

  For example, suppose you have a long list of user interface glitches to clear up. You both know how to do it. It's straightforward and you could go twice as fast independently. Divide and conquer.
- When you need to perform UI Design

  6-up techniques and others allow for collaborative UI ideation but design sometimes benefits from the thought and coherent vision of a single individual.
- When you need brain or physical space

  We all get sick of each other from time to time and pair programming can involve a great deal of time sharing someone's personal space. Get some time apart.

Driving vs. Navigating

Role of the Driver

The driver typically has hands on the keyboard and will be thinking of how to solve the immediate problem. When practicing Test-Driven Development (TDD), the driver will write a test or implement code with the objective of making a test pass. If you are driving and you do not know what to do next, your pair has probably let you down. In this case, suggest writing a test and maybe switching roles.

Most everyone who can program to some degree knows how to play the driver role in a pair. Everyone can benefit from practice. The most difficult aspect of driving is speaking about what you are doing while you are doing it. The second most difficult thing to learn is how to give up control and switch.

Navigator

Most developers need to practice navigation in a pair context to become skilled. Experienced developers who have never paired will have learned to navigate by themselves but may not be accustomed to speaking about it, to guiding someone else or to performing the role so consciously.

Navigation usually consists of asking (aloud!) and often answering such questions as:

- "Where are we?"

- "What is the next step here?

The Navigator constantly assesses progress toward the feature or objective and helps correct course when necessary.

The Navigator may also:

- help the driver get unstuck
- research needed information (eg. api usage, candidate gems, resolve confusion about requirements)
- question the approach
- handle interruptions (run interference)
- point out unseen problems or errors

Switching Roles

Two skilled developers who are evenly matched in terms of ability will often fight for control. You know a pair is really working well when keyboard control shifts back and forth by the minute. If you observe a pair over 5 minutes and do not see the control change hands, something is probably wrong.

If you are the one on the keyboard and find that you have been typing or using the keyboard for 5 minutes straight, or if you notice your pair has disengaged, back away from the keyboard for a moment. Say, "hey, you do this!" Or, "can you take over?"

If you are the one who is supposed to be navigating but you are losing the plot and having trouble seeing the big picture, ask to drive and let the other person navigate for a bit.

TDD Ping-pong

A more structured approach which works well with Test-Driven Development is to take turns writing a test and switching roles to let the other person write the code to implement the test. They would then write the next test and pass control back to you to implement the code. Rinse and repeat.

Respect Your Pair

Pairing requires etiquette. You need to be nice. Most of this is "common sense" but some requires practice – especially if you have never worked in a very collaborative environment.

- Check your ego at the door

  This is the first rule. Don't put anyone down or insult them. You are not a genius and even if you are, you probably don't want to act like one. Put your ego away. If you do a great job pairing, you both did a great job. If you did poorly, blame is shared.
- Ask your pair to explain his or her thinking

  If your driver has gone quiet, ask them to explain what they are doing. If you don't know why the driver is doing something or why the navigator is recommending a certain approach, ask them to explain their thinking.

- Give good criticism

  Be constructive. If you see a problem with the code, say something. Don't just sit their like a lump on a log.

- Take criticism well

  Do not be defensive. All code is collectively owned. It is not "mine" or "yours" – it's ours.

- Do not be silent

  Silence is deadly. When observing a room of pair-programmers, one should hear constant chatter.

  Old habits die hard and most of us learned to program in absolute blissful solitude. Most of us cultivated techniques for tuning others out. That doesn't work here.

- Do not hog the keyboard

  Even if you are not aggressive, your pair may be too timid or intimidated to ask for control. If you've been typing away furiously like you're the only one there, stop. Take your hands off and ask the other person to pick up and carry on.

Change Position!

Pairing involves sitting at a slight angle to the center of the main screen. At ÆLOGICA we have special custom made tables which encourage each member of the pair to direct their chair properly toward the common focus of attention.

If you sit in the same pair position (on either of the left or right side) day after day, the slight asymmetry in your posture and seating position will accumulate. Even if you carefully avoid asymmetrical postures, you will cancel out any accumulated asymmetry by switching positions often.

I believe that moving positions may offer other benefits besides those related to posture and purely physical concern. Changing positions or workstations or even rooms, can help make things feel "fresh" and can help break poor habits or modalities of interaction that set up between team members.

Use Proper Sitting Posture

If you notice that your neck is slightly turned, adjust your chair so that your body faces the screen and your head is positioned straight ahead most of the time.

Over-use of the adjunct or personal laptop can cause asymmetrical posture. When you turn to use a laptop adjacent to your workstation, turn completely to face the laptop using the rotational capability of the chair. If you simply twist your body or your neck, you will end up with neck and back pain. If you twist this way in one direction for a week, you will be miserable. Don't do it.

If you find you need to use your laptop extensively, it may be time to "split" from your pair for a while. Go find a comfortable place to use your laptop where you have more space or where you won't be tempted to sit at an angle or in a twisted position.

Pair Flow

Earlier in the chapter on Maximizing Productivity, we discussed the concept of Flow as it relates to the activity of programming. When you work as a pair, you no longer have freedom to get in the "zone" quite the same way as you would if you were working alone. However, some have described a state called "Pair Flow" – wherein the pair is deeply absorbed in the task. This can be very powerful. You know you are in pair flow when the work feels sticky, and you do not want to get up and you see that your partner feels the same.

Structuring Breaks

When pairing, you want to be diligent about taking breaks. Absorption in the task waxes and wanes for either partner and when you feel like taking a break, the other party may be deep in the problem and not want to break. Out of concern for the pair, you may stick with it and by the time you are absorbed, the your pair may be ready for a break. He or she may then be reluctant to leave and you can find yourself "stuck" to the workstation much too long.

If this happens, try practicing Pomodoro together. We

describe the Pomodoro technique in Maximizing Productivity.

When you take a break while pairing, it is especially important that you get up and get out of the room. Get a little space and time away from your pair. Let them take care of personal business or visit the restroom.

Estimate your work in terms of Pomodoros. Use the chance to co-estimate with your partner. The better you can get at estimating granlar tasks in terms of well-defined blocks of time such as Pomodoros that fit within your break schedule, the more accurate your overall estimates will be. Hours often seem to be too large to use for estimation while minutes are of course too small.

Bookend your end your breaks with with the questions advised in the chapter on Maximizing Productivity. When working with a pair, you really have no excuse. Before you break, ask, "What did we just do?" or "Where are we now?" Then state to your pair what you will start with when you come back. If you are really deep in a problem, leave a note on the screen or on paper as to where you left off.

Keep Each Other Accountable

Mutual accountability is one the great reasons we pair program. With someone programming shoulder to shoulder with us, we have to stay on our toes.

Be explicit about your intentions. Speak out loud. Do not just start typing away. Tell your pair what you are planning to do and why. This alone will have a positive regulating effect on your efficiency.

Keep your momentum up. When you feel like you are slowing down or losing steam, ask your pair to take over. Usually the feeling will pass. You know you did a great job when you are both slightly exhausted and amazed at what you accomplished at the end of the day.

Mind your pair. If your pair is goofing-off too much, wasting time, arriving late, or doing something that detracts from your mutual enthusiasm for the work, or from the productivity of the team, call them out. Do not suffer in silence or try to pick up their slack and make up for their deficiency.

Go to your manager or ask another person outside your team for advice if you have trouble with a difficult pair partner. Chances are you will have some good suggestions. Ultimately if you just cannot stand your pair, your manager may be able to reassign one of you.

What to Do if Your Workplace Does Not Pair

Pairing is a cultural thing. Some cultures do not support it. Some will be actively hostile to the idea. If you work in an office where developers all wear headphones or close their doors you many not have much luck with pairing at first. Management may not be the only obsticle here.

I suggest starting by making sure your own workspace can support pairing and even looks inviting to a potential pair-partner. Make sure you have a large enough desk to accommodate an extra chair. See if you can pull an extra chair in or keep it to the side so you can pair opportunistically with a minimum of fuss. Keep an extra keyboard and mouse handy. If you are running multiple smaller monitors or even a single small one, request a single 27" or larger monitor and swap any little ones out. Pairing works best with a single screen. Keep your desk clean of personal clutter so that someone does not feel that they are invading your personal space too much.

If you do have an office with a door that closes, you're in luck. You may be able to arrange your desk to better support pairing by placing it against a wall rather than facing the door.

If you want to ease into it, volunteer use of your workstation for code review – either to review your own code or that of a colleague.

More suggestions can be found in the chapter "Debug Your Workplace."

Debug Your Workplace

You are responsible for your productivity and your happiness. As you advance and exercise leadership, you will be responsible for the productivity and happiness of others who do the same type of work.

Look around you. Is your workplace conducive to doing good work?

Here is a quick checklist of what you need in your work environment:

1. Quiet
2. Adequate workspace accommodative of a guest for pairing or code review
3. Powerful computer
4. Large monitor
5. Decent internet
6. Whiteboard or glass surface for dry-erase
7. Convenient restrooms
8. Appropriate temperature/climate control

Some things that are nice to have:

1. Natural Light

2. Team rooms accommodating 2 - 4 developers
3. Convenient pantry or break area
4. Convenient restrooms
5. Use of a nearby meeting room

It is a bad sign if your workspace has:

1. Noisy non-technical people located nearby
2. Telephone rings, conversation or intercom noise
3. Open plan offices where you are in a high-traffic area
4. A dungeon-like quality
5. Small, cheap monitors or underpowered hardware

If you observe any of these bad signs or are missing important requirements, it is likely that the technical department or software development team does not have enough pull or perceived importance within the organization to command the resources appropriate to your work. Ask once to address these concerns and plan to look for another job if they are not addressed to your satisfaction. Consider it a litmus test of your bosses. They may not understand right away but if you show them these lists and this chapter, they should at least try to accommodate you as it reflects directly on their status within the organization if they cannot provide necessary resources to their team.

Some companies are genuinely strapped for cash and space. Office space in some cities costs a fortune and usually the CFO and HR tend to do the space planning. Real estate is a precious commodity and office politics often determine which groups get the choicest space. If you decide to put up with sub-par working conditions, do so only if you feel the place offers other overwhelming benefits such as working with highly-skilled people from whom you learn alot.

At a minimum, a team of 4 developers should have at least 200 square feet of space for their immediate work area if they are pairing most of the time. Add 50% if they are not pairing at all. They should have a roughly equivalent amount of common area devoted to or allocated to them. Pair workstations are more space-efficient if you pair much of the time but that doesn't mean you should be packed in like sardines. Common areas and glass walls or windows can help make smaller spaces feel less cramped while still creating spaces for collaboration. If you regularly collaborate with remote team members or clients, team rooms with doors that shut are a must.

When interviewing for a job, ask to see the workplace and get a tour. Observe all of the qualities mentioned here to see how it stacks up. A place that values your talent and is adequately capitalized or profitable will display that in the environment offered and they will be proud to show it off. If they refuse to show you, take a pass.

If you are in the fortunate position to be able to influence the design of a workspace for software developers, take these concerns into consideration. Small mistakes here can have a big impact on the performance of the team and your ability to recruit top talent.

Have Fun

Enjoy your chosen profession. You are in a unique place and time in history. Software development skills are in demand globally and will remain so for the forseeable future. Talented developers around the world enjoy a wide array of employment and economic opportunities.

Strategically, you should locate yourself in a large metro area where there will be the widest array of tech employment. Be ready to relocate for opportunity. Only move to a weaker market for lifestyle reasons or to support a spouse's career. Be honest about the tradeoff. If you are unable to situate in a strong market or live somewhere with a reasonable commute to the business district, focus on opportunities that allow for remote work.

Enjoy Your Work

Find things about your work and your coworkers that you enjoy. Avoid negative people and negative thinking. Contribute to your company culture. Stay optimistic. Do not stress yourself out over minor issues. In any situation, ask yourself, what is the worst that could happen? Maybe you would have to look for a new job.

Keep your resume up to date. Connect to people on LinkedIn. Keep up your blog. Make friends in other companies. Stay in touch with your college friends. Participate in professional community and enthusiast events. Over the course of your career, you will at some point lean on your network for opportunity or advancement.

Stay focused on creating value. Climb the abstraction ladder. Keep your knowledge fresh. Stay on top of trends if you can. If you slip behind for a few years, do not worry. New technology trains leave the station with regularity every couple years. All you have to do is pick a new thing that is gaining traction and jump on board. You will have several more opportunities to get in on the ground floor of a hot trend.

Enjoy Your Life

Strive for a work-life balance. Find things to do after work that involve getting away from a screen. Spend time outdoors. Get away on weekends. Stay healthy.

Travel. Broaden your mind and your experience. Understanding other people better will make you a better developer.